Enduring to the End

Jehovah's Witnesses and Bible Doctrine

Enduring to the End

Jehovah's Witnesses and Bible Doctrine

REGULAR BAPTIST PRESS
1300 North Meacham Road
Schaumburg, Illinois 60173–4888

12773 127173

To my wife, Martha, because of her love for the
Bible, the Word of God

Unless otherwise indicated, all Scripture references are from
the King James Version of the Bible.

ENDURING TO THE END: JEHOVAH'S WITNESSES AND
BIBLE DOCTRINE
© 1987
Regular Baptist Press
Schaumburg, Illinois
Printed in the U.S.A.

Library of Congress Cataloging-in-Publication Data

Hartog, John, 1936–
  Enduring to the end.

  Bibliography: p.
  1. Jehovah's Witnesses—Controversial literature.
I. Title.
BX8526.5.H37   1987   289.9'2   87–4814
ISBN   0–87227–118–8

CONTENTS

"But he that shall endure unto the end, the same shall be saved."

Matthew 24:13

FOREWORD

PERHAPS you have always wondered about Jehovah's Witnesses—What do they believe? When and how did they begin? And what kinds of things do you need to know when they come to your front door?

John Hartog has written this book to answer these kinds of questions. He has ably researched the doctrinal position of the Witnesses, he has clearly set it forth, and he has definitely refuted it with true Biblical exposition.

Dr. Hartog has devoted a separate chapter to each of the ten areas of theology (including the Person and work of God, the Person and work of Christ, the Holy Spirit, the Trinity, and Satan and the angels) and in so doing has provided a systematic analysis of this contemporary sect against the background of Scriptural teaching.

All believers should be aware of the social and religious culture in which they live and work.

Both in the workplace and in the neighborhood, they will have contact with lost men and women who may be entrenched within a cult, and who need to be rescued from their error and moral guilt. In order to have an effective evangelistic outreach, Christians need to have a book like this one in their home libraries. They need to read it and study it. They will then be better prepared to give a reasoned defense of Biblical convictions to those who ask for a reason for their hope (1 Pet. 3:15).

I commend John Hartog for his writing and Regular Baptist Press for its publication of this fine volume. May God grant it a good circulation whereby believers will be edified and challenged to have a positive witness to those who call themselves Jehovah's Witnesses.

May all who read this book profit from Paul's exhortation:

Walk in wisdom toward them that are without, redeeming the time.

Let your speech be alway with grace, seasoned with salt, that ye may know how ye ought to answer every man (Col. 4:5, 6).

Robert Gromacki
Chairman, Bible Department
Cedarville College

PREFACE

WHO has not heard of the Jehovah's Witnesses? They are known by name everywhere. Due to their zeal, they have become a major factor in the modern religious scene.

This book is a study of the history and theology of the Witnesses. The major part of the book is an attempt to present Witness doctrines organized according to the ten areas of systematic theology. This is no easy task. The Witnesses do not publish a true systematic theological work of their own. Their book *Let God Be True* has been helpful, but it is not a systematic theology per se. Books dealing with the Jehovah's Witnesses, while also enlightening, do not have this as an established objective. The two most helpful here have been *Apostles of Denial* by Edmond C. Gruss and *Jehovah's Witnesses* by Anthony Hoekema. In seeking to present Witness theology, the majority of quotations have been taken from the

Witnesses' own books and magazines.

While the primary purpose of this book has not been to refute Witness doctrines (both Gruss and Hoekema have done an excellent piece of work in this area), it has been the author's endeavor to point out where the Witnesses deviate from orthodoxy. It will be seen that these deviations are both serious and numerous.

John Hartog II

PART I

*The Importance
and History
of the Witnesses*

"JW membership in this country has increased by 45% over the past decade."
The Washington Post,
October 3, 1982

1

GROWING LIKE A WEED

THIS week Jehovah's Witnesses will make another three million back calls on homes around the world, which they are trying to convert to their cause. If the number of new doors knocked at was listed, the figure would be far greater. It is conservative to estimate that an average of ten homes a week is called upon by each active Witness. This means that some five million homes in the United States alone are reached weekly by the Witnesses. The number of calls they make every year is greater than the number of people living in the entire United States.

It is because of this colossal effort that the Witnesses are one of the fastest-growing religious bodies in the nation, if not in the world. And this growth is taking place all over the world. Over a period of about twenty-five years prior to 1955, "the Witnesses multiplied internationally by more than fifteen hundred percent."[1]

A look at some checkpoints will reveal this growth. At the turn of the century, there were some 35,000 "Associated Bible Students," as they were then called.[2] The movement at that time was twenty years old. In the 1920s, after another twenty-year period had passed, the cult went through a period of decline as Joseph F. Rutherford sought to gain stronger control over the movement. Many left the fold.[3] (See also appendix, page 169). However, after the consolidation took place, the number began to increase again. Thus after another twenty years, when Nathan H. Knorr took over in 1942, there were slightly over 115,000 members.[4]

The last forty years have seen a phenomenal growth. "In 1961 the average number of active Jehovah's Witnesses throughout the world was 884,587."[5] By 1973 the number of active Witnesses worldwide was 1,656,673.

As of January 1973, the Watchtower Bible and Tract Society (founded in 1896), which is the focal point of the organization, operated in more than 207 lands and sponsored kingdom preaching in the United States alone by more than 483,430 Witnesses. The worldwide membership of Jehovah's Witnesses is in excess of 1,600,000 and attendance at its international assemblies has risen to 3,526,000. In 1972, they sponsored 1,146,328 home Bible studies, spent 267,581,120 hours witnessing, and made 121,226,605 back calls on homes they were attempting to convert.[6]

In the last ten years the pace has continued unabated. There are now 2,500,000 Witnesses knocking on the world's doors. This year alone the Witnesses will have spent more than a third of a *billion* hours witnessing from door to door. When we contemplate the effect of such a zealous, sustained proselyting effort against Christendom, the importance of the movement cannot be denied.

**CHARTING THE GROWTH
OF THE WITNESSES (in thousands)**

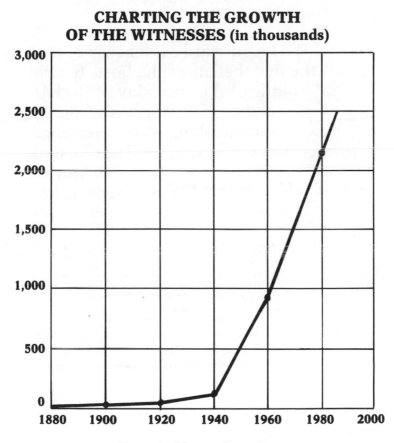

Years in 20-year increments

"The outward evidences are that the marshalling of the hosts for the battle of the great day of God Almighty, is in progress while the skirmishing is commencing."
Charles Taze Russell,
The Watchtower,
January 1886, p. 817

2

HOW IT ALL BEGAN

JEHOVAH'S Witnesses like to trace their movement back to Abel, the son of Adam and Eve, but it was actually founded by Charles Taze Russell in the late 1800s. Charles was born to Joseph L. and Anna Eliza Russell on February 16, 1852. He spent most of his early years in Pittsburgh and Allegheny, Pennsylvania.[1] His parents were Presbyterians of Scotch-Irish descent, and he was reared a staunch Calvinist. Russell's youth was dominated by religious thoughts, especially morbid pictures of hell and final damnation. In fact, as a boy, he would go around Pittsburgh on Saturday nights writing chalk signs on fences to warn people to attend church Sunday that they might escape the torments of eternal fire.

At the age of fifteen Russell was already in partnership with his father, operating a chain of men's clothing stores in and around Allegheny and Pittsburgh. By this time "he had joined the

Congregational church, finding it more to his liking than the Presbyterian."[2] At this time he was a zealous but poorly taught student of the Bible.

At the age of sixteen he tried to win an infidel friend to Christianity. Instead, his friend so completely routed Russell's faith that Russell became a skeptic. His fiery orthodoxy now became frigid unbelief. The doctrines that gave him the greatest problems were those of predestination and eternal punishment.

Russell might well have lived out his life as an agnostic clothing merchant had it not been for the Adventist movement. In 1870, at the age of eighteen, his religious life was deeply affected a second time when he entered a dingy, dusty basement near his Allegheny clothing store and found there a meeting of some Adventists in progress.

Millerite Influence

We must now leave Russell for a moment and go back in history forty more years to a Baptist lay preacher named William Miller. Miller, a former deist who had been converted by reading the Scriptures, became convinced that the return of Christ was near. He began preaching in Dresden, New York in 1831 and a revival followed. He soon became a much demanded speaker. In 1836 he published his first book, *Evidences from Scripture and History of the Second Coming of Christ about the Year 1843: Exhibited in a Course of Lectures.* Many others then joined his movement.

The date of the expected return was refined by Miller on January 1, 1843. He now stated that it would be between March 21, 1843 and March 21, 1844. When March 21, 1844 came and the Lord did not return, Miller was honest enough to admit that he had been wrong. He wrote to his fifty thousand followers, "I confess my error and acknowledge my disappointment."[3]

Miller's followers, however, did not accept the error. After the March 21 date had passed, Samuel S. Snow stated that Miller had been right but the date was to be October 22, 1844 instead. The excitement again built as the day approached. Once again the date-setting scheme failed. This last failure is known in Adventism as the "Great Disappointment."

The Great Disappointment left the Adventists in chaos. New leaders arose with new theories that did not rightly interpret the Scriptures. Miller refused to set another date, stating in 1849, "We expected the personal coming of Christ at that time; and now to contend that we were not mistaken is dishonest. We should never be ashamed frankly to confess our errors. I have no confidence in any of the theories that grew out of the movement."[4] Miller died a Baptist and continued to hold to the imminent return of Christ.

Nevertheless, the theories that Miller repudiated became the bases of the more than fifty denominational groups that were spawned by Miller's movement. Some of these were his direct heirs, some were indirect. They range from the Seventh-day Adventist Church to the General Conference of the Church of God, Armstrong's Worldwide Church of God, the Assemblies of Yahweh and the Jehovah's Witnesses.

The link between Miller's Adventism and the Jehovah's Witness movement is to be found in the Advent Christian Church, formed by groups of

Miller's followers. The forerunners of this denomination were three Millerites, John T. Walsh, Jonathan Cummings and George Storrs. Walsh taught that the wicked dead would be annihilated, that the Millennium was already past and that saints were now in a waiting period for the Lord's return. Cummings taught that Miller was right in his method of determining the time of the Lord's return but was ten years off in his calculations, and that Christ would return in 1854 instead. Storrs taught that the soul is not immortal and that the souls of the righteous dead sleep in an unconscious state in the grave.

When 1854 came and the Lord did not return the Adventists faced another failure. Then a small group of the Adventists rallied behind Jonas Wendell who once again revised the date to 1874. It was four years before this date that Charles Taze Russell dropped into that dingy basement near his Allegheny clothing store and first came in contact with the Adventists. He joined Wendell's group.[5]

Here Russell was taught the doctrine of the "nonexistence of eternal punishment, the second coming of Christ and Biblical chronology."[6] He was also taught the doctrine of soul-sleep. Because it teaches the doctrine of eternal punishment, Russell had not been able to believe the Bible. But with this new system of teaching, Russell's faith in the Bible was in a measure restored.

It is in this Adventist background that we find some of the core doctrines of Jehovah's Witness theology to this day. A study of current Witness theology will reveal a denial of hell, an emphasis on a second coming of Christ, a peculiar system of Biblical chronology, a stress on eschatology (the doctrine of end-time events), a belief in the inspiration of Scripture, a belief in soul-sleep and a denial of the immortality of the soul.

Russell's Early Work

Russell's interest in Bible study was now re-aroused, and he got together some of his business and social friends to study the Bible along with the Adventist group. They met in Pittsburgh from 1870 until 1875. This study group elected him "pastor," although he had never had any theological training, and he was affectionately known by this title among his followers to the day of his death.

Thus it was that the year 1874 came and went and another projected date had failed to be the one in which Christ returned. The disappointment led to dissension over the manner of Christ's second advent. Russell and his faction maintained that Christ had indeed come in 1874 but that His coming was a spiritual or invisible one. Already we see a diminishing of the importance of the great doctrines of Christology.

In 1876 Russell and his faction joined Nelson H. Barbour of Rochester, New York. Barbour was the leader of another group of Adventists who had left the main movement because they felt Christ's second coming was to be a spiritual, in-visible one.

From 1876 to 1878 Russell was the editor of *The Herald of the Morning,* which Barbour had previously published but which had gone defunct. It began anew as a joint venture.[7] Another publication of the joint groups was a book called *Three Worlds or Plan of Redemption.* Published in 1877, this book taught that Christ's second presence had begun invisibly in the fall of 1874. This event was held to be the commencement of a forty-year harvest period, and the times of the Gentiles were to end in 1914. Since then 1914 has been held to be a most significant year in Witness chronology.[8]

The alliance with Barbour was not destined to last, however, for Russell began teaching that the death of Christ was a ransom price paid for Adam's descendants. This teaching was denied by Barbour. To this very day the idea of a ransom plays a major part in Witness theology.[9] In addition, Barbour had predicted that the Church would go to Heaven in April of 1878, another date-setting scheme that failed. As could be expected, Barbour lost support because of the false prophecy.

In 1879 Russell began a new periodical which he entitled *Zion's Watchtower and Herald of Christ's Presence*. The first issue came out on July 1, 1879, with six thousand copies printed. It was sent free of charge to all of Barbour's subscribers. The response was instantaneous and gratifying. The date of the first issue of the *Watchtower* is usually used for the beginning of the Jehovah's Witness movement.

By 1880 some thirty congregations had been formed, spreading across seven different states. A year later, in 1881, Zion's Watchtower Tract Society was formed with Russell as its head. This society was granted a legal charter on December 13, 1884 and was organized as a religious corporation.

Eighteen eighty-six saw the publication of

Russell's book entitled *The Plan of the Ages*. This book was the foundation of all his later theology. It was also the first of his "Millennial Dawn" series which gave the early movement its name. Russell published six books in the series. A seventh, published in 1917 after his death, caused a split among his followers. The series was later called *Studies in the Scriptures* and is still published by some of the splinter groups of Russell's movement.

At first the local congregations were formed by followers of Russell who had read his publications. As time went on he engaged the service of "colporteurs" who spent part or all of their time selling his books and keeping sixty-four percent of the price for their discount. A step toward more formal organization was taken in 1894, when the central office began to pay traveling preachers called "pilgrims" to minister to the various local congregations.

The group had internal struggles from its early days. "In 1893 several prominent members of the Society tried to wrest control from Russell."[10] They were unsuccessful.

Russell's Later Years

From 1893 onward Russell's life was one of trials and scandals. In 1879 he had married Maria F. Ackley. In the early period of their marriage she was quite active in Russell's work, even writing articles for his magazine. However, after the early 1890s difficulties began to build up, and she finally left him in 1897. He continued to support her until 1903. Three years later she sued for divorce because of an improper relationship with a certain Rose Ball. "He denied the truth violently until, when cornered, he admitted embarrassing circumstances."[11] However, the divorce was not granted because of adultery but because of his conceit and domineering spirit, which had made life intolerable for his wife. Thousands left the movement because of his divorce.

Later he "was dragged into court again because he practiced fraud upon his wife. He transferred his property to corporations and societies over which he himself had absolute control, and thus he tried to avoid paying his former wife alimony."[12] At one point J. F. Rutherford and four other Bible students raised $10,000 to pay back alimony in order to save him from further court action.[13]

In 1908 Rutherford, the Society's legal counselor and later second president, obtained property for the society in Brooklyn, New York. It was the old Henry Ward Beecher home. Though the house has long been outgrown, the movement's headquarters still remains in Brooklyn and is referred to as Bethel.

During 1912 Russell made a rapid world tour to such places as Japan and China. Upon coming back he denounced the Christian mission agencies for warring competition. When pinned down, however, he admitted he had not seen many missionaries. His whole stay in Japan had been but a few days' duration.

Probably the most famous scandal of the period was his "miracle wheat." Russell claimed it would out-produce ordinary wheat fivefold. This scandal was exposed by *The Brooklyn Daily*

Eagle in 1913. Russell sued for libel. The U.S. government investigated the wheat and found it to be slightly less productive than ordinary wheat. Russell lost the suit.

Russell was a man of great energy and great conceit. He announced in the opening pages of his *Studies in the Scriptures* that it was better to read his comments on the Bible and omit Bible reading than to read the Bible and omit his comments.

From the beginning, the date of 1914 was prominent in Russell's theology. He taught that the gospel age ended in 1874 and that that year marked the dawning of the millennial age. This "Millennial Dawn" period was to be a harvest time of forty years. During this period the Jews were to have returned to Palestine, the Gentile nations were to have been overthrown and 1914 would see the glorification of the saints with the establishment of God's direct rule on earth. At that time mankind was to be restored to perfection on earth.

Nineteen fourteen, of course, did not bring the end of the age. What it did bring was World War I. The Russellites latched onto that event as proof that the beginning of the end had occurred. But even Russell himself became worried as the predicted year drew near, so he revised the date to 1918. He did not live long enough to see the revised date also fail.[14]

During his lifetime, the Jehovah's Witness movement got its theology from him and much of this teaching has filtered down to the present.

As a speaker, Russell swayed many; as a theologian he impressed no one competent; as a man, he failed before the true God. Russell traveled extensively, spoke incessantly, and campaigned with much energy for "a great awakening" among the people of the world. In the course of his writings and lectures Russell denied many of the cardinal doctrines of the Bible—the Trinity, the Deity of Christ, the physical Resurrection and Return of Christ, eternal punishment, the reality of Hell, the eternal existence of the soul and the validity of the infinite Atonement, to state a few.[15]

Russell was active to the end of his life. On October 31, 1916, he died on board a transcontinental train as it neared Pampa, Texas. He was on his way home from a California speaking trip. The funeral oration was delivered by "Judge" Joseph F. Rutherford, who proved himself worthy of the occasion. He stated that Russell did not sleep in death, "but was instantly changed from the human to the divine nature, and is now forever with the Lord."[16]

How did the Jehovah's Witness movement begin? It began with Charles Taze Russell, who had come to deny many of the doctrines long held by orthodox Christians and clearly taught in the Bible. By the time of his death in 1916, the legal and doctrinal foundation of the Society had been firmly established.[17]

"We should not, therefore, expect the Lord's second coming to be in a body visible to human eyes."
Judge Rutherford,
The Harp of God, p. 225

———

"Behold, he cometh with clouds; and every eye shall see him. . . ."
Revelation 1:7

3

THE JUDGE CARRIES ON

THE second president of the Witnesses was Joseph F. "Judge" Rutherford, who ruled the Society from 1917 to 1942. Joseph Franklin Rutherford was born on November 8, 1869 in Booneville, Missouri. His parents were Baptists. When he was sixteen he entered college to study law. At the age of twenty-two he was admitted to the bar and began to practice law, later serving as public prosecutor for Booneville. Still later he was appointed a special judge for the Fourteenth Judicial District of Missouri.[1]

In 1894, at the age of twenty-five, he first came into contact with members of the Watchtower Society. He purchased several volumes of Russell's *Studies in the Scriptures* and began studying these with his wife.[2] Twelve years later, in 1906, he joined the movement, and the following year he became the Society's legal adviser.

As mentioned previously, Rutherford was

mainly responsible for the obtaining of the Brooklyn property in 1908. He also served as Russell's personal attorney. His rise to a place of prominence in the movement is further confirmed by the fact that he was the one who delivered Russell's funeral sermon.

The Power Struggle

Rutherford, however, was not the only one to lay claim to the official leadership of the Society. A leading opponent was Paul S. L. Johnson, who had been given "enlarged powers" by Russell. Nevertheless, at the corporation meeting of January 6, 1917, two months after Russell's death, Rutherford was elected the second president of the Watchtower Society.

The two years following the death of Russell were critical ones for the Society. A power struggle developed between Rutherford and Johnson and other board members as to who should control the Society. Johnson and four of the board members were attempting to make the entire board the governing body, whereas Rutherford wanted that prerogative for himself.

In July of his first year as president, the book *The Finished Mystery* was published under Rutherford's direction. It was chiefly a commentary on Ezekiel and Revelation compiled by Watchtower editors from Russell's writings. The book was another source of trouble among board members. "The book broadened the gap in the Bethel headquarters, caused much dissension in the local congregations, and paved the way for governmental action against the Witnesses."[3]

The Finished Mystery was billed as the sev-

enth volume of *Studies in the Scriptures* and as
the posthumous work of Pastor Russell. The book
stated that Russell was the man clothed in linen
with the writer's inkhorn by his side of Ezekiel 9:3–
11, the "faithful and wise servant" of Matthew
24:45–47 and "the angel of the church of the
Laodiceans" of Revelation 3:14. Nevertheless,
many of the Bible Students, as they were then
called, immediately rose up to denounce the book
as a departure from Russell's teachings.

Before Johnson and the other board members could act against him, Rutherford, having
been trained in law, found a loophole in the
Society's charter and deposed them (1918). He
also began to purge the Brooklyn headquarters
of any who opposed him. Because of the purge,
and the unrest within the Society, a number of
splinter groups formed and many left the movement. The Dawn Bible Students Association was
one of these groups as was the Layman's Home
Missionary Movement. Both of these have continued down to the present. They hold to Russell's
theology more closely than do the present day
Witnesses.

If the board had gained control, the Society
would likely have remained closer to Russell's
theology. With Rutherford in charge, certain
changes in theology appeared as he sought to
wean the Society from Russell and graft it to himself. He stressed a progressive revelation and
"new light." Both the dissension and the idea of
progressive revelation, as well as a de-emphasis
of Russell's importance, can be seen in the following excerpt from the 1969 Witness book called,
Then is Finished the Mystery of God:

Those who chose to follow a dead man left the ranks. Those who believed that the light of Bible truth did not stop advancing with the death of the first president of the Watchtower Bible & Tract Society held to God's visible organization [i.e., the Jehovah's Witnesses] and continued searching the Holy Scriptures in the advancing light.[4]

The Finished Mystery not only caused dissension within the Society, it caused trouble without as well. It contained many antiwar statements, which brought the U.S. government into the picture. In May 1918, warrants were issued for the arrest of Rutherford and seven other Society leaders, charging them with conspiring to cause refusal of duty in the armed forces. "On June 20 the eight were found guilty of these charges, and the next day they were sentenced to twenty years imprisonment in the federal penitentiary at Atlanta, Georgia."[5]

The prison term only served to make Rutherford and the other leaders martyr-heroes to the movement. Rutherford became more bitter in his attack on government and religious organizations, since he felt the clergy and the government had acted in conjunction in putting them in prison.

In the spring of 1919, after the war had ended, the Witness leaders were released, and in 1920 the indictments against them were dropped. Upon release from prison, Rutherford found only a skeleton of the organization remaining. This was to his advantage. He reorganized the Society to his liking and became more and more the controller of the movement. "Throughout the years following Russell's death, Rutherford rose in power and popularity among the 'Russellites' and to oppose him was tantamount to questioning the authority of Jehovah Himself."[6]

That Rutherford was successful in his drive for power can be seen in the following statement by Mead:

> Three corporations eventually controlled the society: the Watchtower Bible and Tract Society of Pennsylvania, the Watchtower Bible and Tract Society of New York, and the International Bible Student's Association of England. The Judge, however, was the actual ruling power.[7]

Rutherford's drive for power not only affected his relationship to the board, it affected the corporate Society's relationship to the individual congregations as well. Under Russell, the local assemblies had been independent. Rutherford worked consistently to bring them under the control of the Brooklyn headquarters. He used many tactics including persuasion and threats. Those who opposed him were classified automatically in the Evil Slave class, which meant that they had no hope of eternal life. This threat in itself brought many to fall in line behind him.

In Russell's time the elders of the local congregations (called companies) had been elected by the individual members. Under Rutherford the theocratic hierarchy was at last realized in 1938, when the individual congregations by resolution signed away their independence. This form of highly authoritarian government marks the Witnesses to this day.

Rutherford further proved that he was in charge by launching a new magazine, *The Golden Age*, on October 1, 1919. This publishing of a new magazine was in explicit contradiction to Russell's wishes. In 1937 its name was changed to *Consolation*, and in 1946 it was changed again to the title by which it is known today—*Awake!*

Rutherford's Writings

Rutherford proved to be an even more prolific author than Russell had been:

> In comparing Russell and Rutherford, it must be noted that the former was a literary pygmy compared to his successor. Russell's writings were distributed, approximately fifteen or twenty million copies of them, over a period of sixty years, but Rutherford's in half that time were many times that amount. The prolific judge wrote over one hundred books and pamphlets, and his works as of 1941 had been translated into eighty languages.[8]

In 1921 the Society published *The Harp of God*, the first of Rutherford's multitudinous books. At first Rutherford followed the Russellite line of thinking closely, but after a few years he began to receive new insights, and slowly Russell's writings and person were forgotten. "Mention Russell's name to a present-day Witness, and as likely as not you will get an uncomprehending stare."[9] However, as Rutherford's books, tracts and pamphlets supplanted those of Russell, and as he began to neglect some of Russell's teachings, dissension became more prevalent.

William J. Schnell, who left the movement

after being at its core, claims that more than
three-fourths of the Bible Students originally in
the movement left Rutherford's group between
1921 and 1931.[10] Gruss, another who left the Witnesses, indicates that by 1931 some forty thousand had left for a variety of reasons.[11]

From 1920 onward, all members of the congregations were given the job of selling and dis-
tributing Watchtower literature and were required to turn in weekly reports of their activities.
Rutherford laid more stress on witnessing to
others than Russell had. However, Rutherford
did continue his predecessor's practice of setting
dates. The first date he set for the coming battle
of Armageddon was 1920. This was later revised
to 1925 and again to 1940.

Rutherford also set up the class system cur-
rently found among the Witnesses. The first class
was the Mordecai-Naomi class, made up of those
who had joined the movement prior to 1922.
These were the 144,000 members who made up
the Body of Christ. However, such large numbers
of this class had become unfaithful and had been
named part of the Evil Slave class that a new class,
the Ruth-Esther class, came into being from 1922
to 1929 to fill in the vacancies.

From 1931 onward, a third class known as the
Jonadabs or Great Multitude was formed. All con-
verts today still become part of this class. Their
hope is not that of being born again and of going
to Heaven, since that elect number is full. Rather,
they are offered the hope of an earthly paradise
on this planet.

With the idea of an earthly paradise ahead,
the prophecies to Israel were reinterpreted and

transferred from literal Israel to spiritual Israel—
the Jehovah's Witnesses.

A New Emphasis

Rutherford, while continuing to deny all the
cardinal doctrines of the Bible that Russell had
denied, shifted the movement's emphasis in a new
direction: the vindication of Jehovah's name. This
is still the primary emphasis of the Witnesses
today. In this area the Witnesses are similar to
eight other heirs of the old Millerite movement
such as the Assemblies of Yahweh and a group
called Workers Together With Elohim.

With this shift, the Witness message centered
more and more on the Jehovah of the Old Testament and less and less on the Christ of the New
Testament. The transition can be seen in several
ways. First, the name of the movement itself was
changed. In 1931, at a convention in Columbus,
Ohio, at the Judge's bidding, the assembled members of the Society adopted a resolution that
from then on they were to be called Jehovah's
Witnesses.[12] This new name was based on the
words of Isaiah 43:10, "Ye are my witnesses, saith
the LORD, and my servant whom I have cho-
sen. . . ."

Second, the transition can be seen in the writings of the movement. In that same year, 1931,
Rutherford produced the book *Vindication,* a
three-volume commentary on Ezekiel. Its main
thrust is that Jehovah will be vindicated. The Witness book, *Let God Be True* (the very title implies
vindication of Jehovah), states that the primary
purpose Christ came to earth was not for man's

salvation but rather for vindication of Jehovah's name:

> To the Jews exclusively he [Jesus] preached, saying: "Repent, for the kingdom of the heavens has drawn near." After this announcement of the Kingdom Jesus went to John, showing the primary purpose for which he came to earth, namely, to bear witness to God's kingdom which will vindicate the sovereignty and holy name of Jehovah God.[13]

Third, this shift can be seen in the renaming of the *Watchtower*. In March of 1939, *The Watchtower and Herald of Christ's Presence* became *The Watchtower Announcing Jehovah's Kingdom*. Thus the name of Christ was played down, and the name of Jehovah was emphasized.

Rutherford taught a progressive revelation, thereby justifying later changes in doctrine. This is why some of his later works do not always agree in interpretation of specific passages with some of his earlier works.

Before leaving Rutherford and his influence on the Witnesses, it should be noted that it was under Rutherford and his hatred for the government that the Witnesses began to refuse to salute the flag. This practice continues today and is justified on the grounds that the flag is an idol.

On January 8, 1942, Rutherford died. He had been the president of the Witness organization for twenty-five years. "When Rutherford died, he left behind him not only a tight-knit, organized 'Theocracy,' but also a self-propagating and self-indoctrinating organization which has complete control over its members."[14]

"There was no resistance or opposition to Knorr's election. This marked the emergence of Jehovah's Witnesses as a modern, full-fledged twentieth-century business corporation."
Chandler W. Sterling,
The Witnesses, pp. 62, 63

4

THE WITNESSES
COME OF AGE

ALTHOUGH the *Yearbook of American and Canadian Churches, 1973* states (evidently from a Witness viewpoint) that the Witnesses "have no human leader,"[1] they continue to have a very strong hierarchy. Their third president was Nathan H. Knorr, another able organizer.

Nathan Homer Knorr was born on April 23, 1905 in Bethlehem, Pennsylvania. His parents were members of the Reformed Church and Knorr was taught Calvinistic doctrine as a child. However, "At the age of sixteen he had already resigned his membership in the Reformed Church and had associated himself with the Allentown, Pennsylvania congregation of Jehovah's Witnesses."[2]

After graduating from high school in 1923, Knorr, then eighteen, joined the staff at the Bethel headquarters in Brooklyn. He was a loyal disciple and a trustworthy and hard-working Society servant. He quickly gained the attention and the confidence of those over him. He was a worker Judge Rutherford could count on, and it was not long before he became the coordinator for all the printing activities. In 1932 he was named general manager of the publishing office and factory. He was twenty-seven at the time.

Two years later, in 1934, Knorr was made director of the New York corporation of the Watchtower Bible and Tract Society, where he also served on the editorial staff. In 1935 he was elected vice-president. In 1940 he was elected vice-president of the Pennsylvania corporation as well. During the last few years of Rutherford's life Knorr actually ran the Brooklyn office. He was certain that he was among the 144,000, the elite group among the Jehovah's Witnesses.

Knorr Elected President

It was no surprise that after Rutherford's death Knorr was elected his successor. "After Rutherford's death [Knorr] was elected president of both American corporations as well as the International Bible Students Association of England. Each of these positions are lifetime."[3] Thus again, as with Rutherford, there was a concentration of power in one man.

Knorr was, by design, less well-known than either Rutherford or Russell had been. However, his success as an administrator was no less spectacular. Whereas there had been 115,000 Witnesses when he became president, there were 2,200,000 when he died.

The reason Knorr was not so well known is

that during his presidency Witness books began to be published anonymously:

> The policy was adopted that all future publications of the Society would be published anonymously. No by-lines on *any* printed materials were to go out under the sponsorship of the Jehovah's Witnesses. This move cut off at the grass roots any possibilty of the growth of a personality cult.[4]

There is little doubt, however, that Knorr had the final word as to what was published. Only Knorr and the few top officials of the corporations knew exactly who wrote the books, magazine articles and tracts put out by the Watchtower.

As Rutherford had treated Russell, so it was done to him:

> Russell's books, as they fell out of print, were not reprinted; and it was Judge Rutherford, not Pastor Russell, who was accepted everywhere as the voice of Jehovah. Now very much the same fate is overtaking Rutherford. *His* books likewise are allowed to fall out of print, and his name is seldom on the lips of any save the older members of the society.[5]

Today, with the passage of another forty years, Rutherford's name has faded completely into the background.

Changes under Knorr

One of the first changes Knorr brought about was the abandonment of Rutherford's sermons on phonograph records, which the Witnesses had played at doorsteps whenever they could. Knorr brought about changes also in the educational program of the Witnesses. Whereas under Rutherford the Witnesses often knew little about the Bible apart from Rutherford's records, Knorr's Witnesses were better trained. He realized that the day had come when every Witness had to learn to speak for himself and the Watchtower.

A year after Knorr took office, the Gilead Watchtower Bible School was established at South Lansing, New York. In 1961 the school was moved to Brooklyn. A prerequisite for entry was that the applicant had to have spent at least two years in full-time witnessing work. Of the many applicants to the school, only the hundred best were selected for each class. Originally the classes ran for five months, but later the course became a ten-month program.

Knorr also established a program of Theocratic Ministry Schools in each Jehovah's Witness assembly. These sought to train the Witnesses in public speaking and mold them into confident, friendly door-to-door salesmen for the Society.

> No one was to go to the front lines of the struggle against the world without being properly armed. There would be no sheep sent forth among the wolves until they were smart enough to know what to do when they were out in Satan's world. They were provided with the twentieth-century weapon of good public relations. They now had their own self-improvement courses designed to turn them into reasonably polished speakers.[6]

In addition to training in public speaking, the

Witnesses were now trained in the use of Bible aids, Witness doctrine, general Bible content and debate. At first this training was restricted to men, but in 1958 the door was also opened to women.

New Books

Under Knorr, as under his predecessors, the publishing of books continued unabated. "This publishing of books explaining the Word of God is one of the outstanding characteristics of the movement."[7] The first book published under Knorr's administration was *The New World* (1942), followed by *The Truth Shall Make You Free* (1943).

It is helpful at this point to review some of the books published under Knorr's presidency. To aid the Witnesses in a general knowledge of the Bible from a Witness viewpoint, two books were published: *Equipped for Every Good Work* (1946) and *All Scripture Is Inspired of God and Beneficial* (1963). The latter is a summary of the contents of the books of the Bible.

Several books also were published to help the Witnesses in their witnessing, among them *Theocratic Aid to Kingdom Publishers* (1945) and *Qualified to Be Ministers* (1955). The latter covers such topics as how to study the Bible, how to conduct meetings and how to witness.

Qualified to Be Ministers also gave the Witnesses a knowledge of the history of the movement. A second book, *Jehovah's Witnesses in the Divine Purpose* (1959) is primarily concerned with the history of the movement as told from a definite Witness viewpoint. Particularly enlightening is chapter 11, which deals with the conflict between Rutherford and the board along with Paul S. L. Johnson (pp. 69–73). The conflict is definitely seen through Rutherford's eyes.

New doctrinal books also were published under Knorr's presidency. These books replaced Rutherford's *The Harp of God* (1921). The first was *Let God Be True* (1946), which is a Jehovah's Witness doctrinal summary. It was revised in 1952 and has been translated into fifty languages. More than 17,000,0000 copies have been distributed. *Make Sure of All Things, Hold Fast to What Is Fine* (1965) serves a similar purpose from a different perspective. A compilation of Scripture passages under 123 topics, this small book serves as a handy Scripture reference guide to Witnesses in their door-to-door witnessing. The verses cited are often taken out of context to prove Witness doctrines. For example, Acts 1:8, "Ye shall receive power, after that the Holy Ghost is come upon you . . ." is cited as proof that the "Holy Spirit is God's Active Force, not a person" (p. 487).

A significant publication in Witness literature was the New World Translation of the Holy Scriptures. The project began in 1950 with the New Testament and was followed by five volumes of the Old Testament (1953–1960). The six were combined in 1961 under the above title. More will be said concerning this volume in the next chapter. Suffice it to say here that the Witnesses use this translation especially in cases where it clearly supports their doctrines when other translations do not, such as for John 1:1 and Hebrews 1:8. In addition to being a tool to convert others, the New World Translation is useful also in the indoctrination of the Witnesses themselves.

There were some minor changes in theology under Knorr but none of any real significance. However, individual Scripture passages were reinterpreted, and sometimes there was even a complete reversal of a former view. Some changes were made in terminology also. For example, although the cross is still referred to as the "torture stake," local assemblies are now called congregations instead of companies. Publishers (i.e., regular full-time workers) came to be called ministers. There was an emphasis on building Kingdom Halls, whereas previously the Witnesses had usually met in homes or in rented halls.

Expansion was another characteristic of the Knorr years. For every Witness there had been when he took over, there were nineteen when he died. This expansion has been especially characteristic on the foreign field. During the time Knorr presided, the work expanded into two hundred nations of the world.

Judge Rutherford had put an end to the use of music in Witness services, considering it to be frivolous. Knorr revived the practice and the first Jehovah's Witness songbook appeared in 1966.

As president, Knorr held absolute power in the Witness Society. Neither the corporation directors nor the board members served as checks or balances on his power. He confidently expected Armageddon to begin by the time he was ready to step down as the last president of the Society.[8] However, Armageddon did not come and Knorr died on June 8, 1977.

Franz Elected

On June 22 of that year the Society's board members elected 83-year-old Frederick W. Franz as the fourth president of the Witnesses. He too was elected president of both the Pennsylvania and New York corporations. Franz had become one of Russell's Bible Students in 1913 when he was about nineteen. Soon after, he dropped out of the University of Cincinnati to throw his lot in with the Witnesses.[9] He eventually became one of the directors and, along with Knorr, made the first official visit for the Society into Mexico and Central America in 1945. Due to his age, his presidency will not be a long one.

This, then, is a history of the movement that was known as Russellism, Millennial Dawnism, The International Bible Students and finally the Jehovah's Witnesses. It began with a lone man who had trouble with some of the fundamental doctrines of Scripture. It now is a way of life for two and a half million people. Russell gave the movement its basic doctrines and set it on its way. Rutherford added some new emphases, consolidated and organized it. Knorr upgraded and expanded it.

Let us now investigate the teachings of this organization that publishes such books as *The Truth that Leads to Eternal Life; Make Sure of All Things, Hold Fast to What Is Fine;* and *This Means Everlasting Life.*

PART II

The Theology
of the Witnesses

". . . in this book, our appeal is to the Bible for truth. Our obligation is to back up what is said herein by quotations from the Bible for proof of truthfulness and reliability."
Watchtower Bible and Tract Society,
Let God Be True, p. 10

"You can 'prove' almost anything from the Bible if you are allowed to select verses or portions of verses as if they told the whole story."
James W. Sire,
Scripture Twisting, p. 80

5

PROVING IT BY THE BIBLE

THE Witnesses make much of their growth statistics. Some have gone so far as to use these growth statistics as a guarantee that they have the truth.[1] However, the same argument could be used for Islam, which in its early years swept over all of North Africa and Spain, invaded the Balkans and marched eastward as far as the islands of southeast Asia. The argument could also be used for communism, which, starting less than a century ago, now dominates one-third of the world's population.

To see whether Witness theology really proclaims the truth, we must study it in the light of God's Word. In so doing, we will organize this analysis of doctrine according to the ten divisions of systematic theology. The first of these is bibliology, the doctrine concerning the Scriptures.

Concerning the inspiration of the Bible, the

Witnesses would fit right in with any fundamental group. The difference lies in interpretation, and there the difference between the Witnesses and fundamentalism is great.

The book, *Make Sure of All Things, Hold Fast to What Is Fine*, referred to previously, is a Scripture reference guide in which verses are arranged under 123 topics. Under these topics there are subtopics which give a clear picture of Witness beliefs in various areas. Under the topic "Bible," the following may be gleaned: First, the Bible is the Word of Jehovah God.[2] This belief is documented by such verses as Exodus 20:1, "God proceeded to speak all these words"; Isaiah 7:7, "This is what the Lord Jehovah has said"; Jeremiah 1:9; John 14:10 and Ephesians 6:17.

Second, the Bible is "inspired of God, not of human origination."[3] To substantiate this belief, 2 Timothy 3:16 and 17 and 1 Thessalonians 2:13 are quoted. The inspiration of the Bible is further explained by the statement, "Men were moved by God's spirit [note the small *s*] to write."[4] At this point 2 Samuel 23:1 and 2; Acts 1:16; 3:21; 28:25 and 2 Peter 1:20 and 21 are given.

Third, the Bible is God's truth. Its divine origin is proved by prophecy. Its truth is shown by the candor of its writers as they recorded their own failures without trying to cover them up. The writers did not glorify themselves but directed glory to God. Here such verses as Psalms 113:3–5 and Revelation 7:12 are given. The truth of the Bible is corroborated by archaeology. It is in harmony with true science. Its preservation in spite of opposition shows it to be God's Word. Those who follow the example of Christ and the apostles cannot view portions of the Bible simply as myths.

Fourth, the Witnesses hold that none of the Bible is out of date; it is all beneficial, including the Old Testament. This belief is upheld by the fact that Jesus and the apostles freely quoted the Old Testament; the Old Testament contains examples for our benefit; and the Bible is a united whole.

Fifth, "Regular Bible reading [is] important" and "Gaining [an] understanding of the Bible [is] vital."[5] At this point it is noted that help is needed in gaining this understanding. The example of Philip and the Ethiopian is cited. "For [a] right interpretation of [the] Bible we must look to God."[6] A right explanation is always in harmony with the rest of God's Word. A grave warning is then given: "Personal interpretation may lead to twisting of Scripture."[7] In the Witness organization all interpretation comes down from the hierarchy. Witnesses are not encouraged to study the Bible for themselves apart from Brooklyn's interpretations. If they did, they would soon cease to be Jehovah's Witnesses.

Sixth, God's written Word is not to be replaced by human traditions. "Scriptures warn against being misled by false religious tradition."[8] To the Witnesses, of course, the Watchtower's doctrinal system is not human tradition. Then comes a warning against adding to or subtracting from Scripture and a note that Scripture must be used honestly.

Seventh, "Jehovah reveals Himself and His purposes through His written Word."[9] This section seeks to promote the New World Translation under the subtopic "Scripture texts that illustrate the improved understanding that results from modern translation."[10] Here difficult verses of the King James Version and the Douay Version are printed side by side with the New World Version.

The Witnesses, then, believe in an inspired Bible. This belief comes through very clearly in Watchtower literature:

> His spirit [note again that small *s*] did work in the Bible's production, as the writers themselves are quick to acknowledge. David said: "The spirit of the LORD spake by me." Luke declared: "He, through the mouth of his holy prophets from of old has spoken." Peter added to the testimony: "No prophecy of Scripture springs from any private release. For prophecy was at no time brought by man's will, but men spoke from God as they were borne along by holy spirit.[11]

The Witnesses certainly do believe that the Bible is inspired of God. They also are not at fault as to the meaning of inspiration. This meaning is made clear in their book *Is the Bible Really the Word of God,* which states:

> The expression "inspired of God" is translated from a Greek word meaning "God-breathed." By "breathing" his own spirit upon faithful men, God moved them to write the Sacred Scriptures.[12]

The Problem

The problem lies not in the Witnesses' view of inspiration but in their system of interpretation. Since the Witnesses regard themselves as spiritual Israel, and the prophecies to Israel are therefore to be applied to the Witnesses, a system of interpretation akin to the allegorical is used. This is in spite of Watchtower claims to have the true interpretation:

> Knowing that God by his holy spirit inspired the Holy Scriptures, thus making them reliable, we choose to let him do the interpreting. How? By his records of fulfilled prophecy and by the things he has caused to occur in modern history to fulfill prophecies due to come to pass in our day. "Doth not interpretation belong to God?" (Genesis 40:8, *Dy*). Yes, and his interpretation is the true one.[13]

Witness hermeneutics, regardless of such claims, lead to some fanciful interpretations. The following sample from the book *Then Is Finished the Mystery of God,* a Watchtower commentary on the book of Revelation, amply illustrates the differences in interpretation. Revelation 11:3–12 speaks of the two witnesses of the end time. They prophesy for 1260 days, are killed by the beast out of the abyss, but after three and one-half days are resurrected and ascend to Heaven. In Witness interpretation the two witnesses turn out to be not two, but a host of people! They are the International Bible Students of 1918:

> Today those remaining of this anointed Remnant are known world wide as Jehovah's Witnesses. They were also his witnesses back there in 1918. They are the ones designated in Revelation 11:3 as "my two witnesses."[14]

As if that were not enough, several pages later the two witnesses turn out to be eight leaders of the movement. The killing of the two witnesses is taken to mean that Rutherford and the other seven leaders were put in prison by the government in 1918. "It killed God's 'two witnesses,' the anointed remnant, as far as their tormenting prophesying 'in sackcloth' was concerned."[15]

The three and one-half days of their death "ended in March of 1919."[16] At this time the eight leaders were set free from prison. Their resurrection was this release from prison and return to Watchtower activity. (No one would ever come to such a conclusion by reading the book of Revelation apart from Witness literature.) "Then, indeed, 'spirit of life from God' entered into the symbolic corpses of the 'two witnesses,' and they became alive to the 'witnessing' activity that now lay ahead of them."[17]

Thus, while saying much about an inspired Bible, the Witnesses nullify it by some of the most fanciful interpretations to be found anywhere. The two witnesses of Revelation were not really two, according to the Witnesses' interpretation, and they were not really killed. The three and one-half days were not really three and one-half days. Their resurrection was not really a resurrection from the dead. As might be expected, "symbolic" is a favorite term of the Watchtower.

Not only do the Witnesses follow fanciful interpretations of the Bible to suit their doctrines, they also use Scripture out of context to try to prove their views. For example, in trying to prove that blood transfusions to preserve present life lead to a loss of eternal life, they cite Matthew 16:25 and 26, "Whoever wants to save his soul will lose it; but whoever loses his soul for my sake will find it. For what benefit will it be to a man if he gains the whole world but forfeits his soul? or what will a man give in exchange for his soul?"[18] These two verses from Matthew have nothing at all to do with blood transfusions. In Christ's day blood transfusions were unknown. But to the Witnesses Matthew 16:25 and 26 prove that anyone who has a blood transfusion automatically loses eternal life.

Hoekema rightly observes:

Instead of listening to Scripture and subjecting themselves wholly to its teachings, as they claim to do, they actually impose their own theological system upon Scripture and force it to comply with their beliefs.[19]

Anyone can prove anything by the Bible by means of an allegorical interpretation and by taking Scripture out of context. The Watchtower is a master in this area.[20]

A New Translation

In the past the Witnesses had problems when they knocked on doors and tried to push their interpretations of Scripture. Eventually they would meet an individual who would take out a Bible and begin looking up verses that disproved Witness views. This was frustrating to the Witnesses. "To them, the words of the older translations did not convey the meaning that they were supposed to."[21] In reality, the older translations did not convey the meaning the Jehovah's Witnesses were reading into the Bible.

To correct this situation, Knorr commissioned some veteran Witnesses to make a new translation of the Bible, the New World Translation of the Holy Scriptures. The problem with this version is not simply that "LORD" is changed to "Jehovah" or even that "cross" is changed to "torture stake"; it goes much deeper:

> Their *New World Translation* of the Bible is by no means an objective rendering of the sacred text into modern English, but is *a biased translation in which many of the peculiar teachings of the Watchtower Society are smuggled into the text of the Bible itself"* (italics in original).[22]

A study of the New World Translation shows that Scriptural texts such as John 1:1 and Hebrews 1:8 have been reworked in such a way that they no longer show the deity of Christ. Likewise, "Holy Spirit" always appears as "holy spirit," with a small *h* and *s*, since the Witnesses teach that He is simply a force. Another classic example of Scripture twisting is the NWT rendering of Colossians 1:15–17. Here the translators added the word "other" four times to make it appear that Christ is a creature and not the Creator.

> He is the image of the invisible God, the first-born of all creation; because by means of him all [other] things were created in the heavens and upon the earth, the things visible and the things invisible, no matter whether they are thrones or lordships or governments or authorities. All [other] things have been created through him and for him. Also, he is before all [other] things and by means of him all [other] things were made to exist (brackets in original) (Col. 1:15–17, NWT).

There is absolutely no basis in the Greek for the addition of this word. Here the Witnesses stand self-condemned, for their own rendering of Revelation 22:18 states, "If anyone makes an addition to these things, God will add to him the plagues that are written in this scroll."

Space does not permit a further analysis of the NWT here. For more on this subject, read *The Jehovah's Witnesses' New Testament* by Robert H. Countess.[23]

The Witnesses also publish an interlinear Greek New Testament. Their first effort along this line was a reprint of *The Emphatic Diaglott* which was originally produced by Benjamin Wilson, the leader of a small cult called the Christadelphians. Witnesses now publish *The Kingdom Interlinear Translation of the Greek Scriptures*. This volume combines the Westcott and Hort Greek text with an English interlinear and a revised New World Translation. Now the Witnesses can confidently back up their views with "The Greek says. . . ."

In summary of Witness bibliology, Lewis correctly states, "Unlike many other cults, the Witnesses do not subscribe to another inspired book in addition to Scripture."[24] However, the Witnesses are like other cults in that they twist the Scriptures to fit their preconceived doctrines.

"The Great Theocrat, the Unfailing
Purposer, the True and
Living God."
Make Sure of All Things, p. 188

"Jehovah's Witnesses worship a
God of vengeance, justice and law
who seems to fit into the Old Testament context better than the
New . . . . The Witnesses tell us
what really arouses the wrath of
God is the failure of Christians to
use his proper name, Jehovah."
William J. Whalen,
Armageddon Around the Corner,
pp. 82 and 83

6

THE GREAT THEOCRAT

THE second doctrine usually covered in systematic theologies is theology proper. Theology proper may be defined as a study of the facts concerning the triune God and the works of God the Father. Normally, theology proper begins by studying the triune God and, after it completes that topic, moves on to deal with the Person and work of God the Father as distinct from the other Persons of the Trinity. However, because of the Witness teachings about Christ and the Holy Spirit, what is said here about God refers for the most part to God the Father alone.

God's Existence

The Witnesses certainly teach the existence of God. In the book, *Things in Which It Is Impossible for God to Lie*, the first chapter is entitled, "God Lives! How We Know It." The chapter uses the four classical arguments for the existence of God: the ontological argument, the cosmological argument, the teleological argument and the anthropological argument. In spite of their scholarly-sounding names, these classic arguments are really quite simple. Let us follow them through the chapter "God Lives!"

First, the portion that deals with the **ontological** argument states that since man everywhere believes in God, there must be a God Who inspired that belief. At this point in the chapter there is a discussion taken from *The Encyclopedia Americana*, which says in part,

> There does not seem to have been a period of history where mankind was without belief in a supernatural author and governor of the universe. The most savage nations have some rudimentary ideas of a god or supreme being. Man is a religious as well as a rational being.[1]

Second, the **cosmological** argument states that every effect must have its cause. In seeking to prove the existence of God, the chapter states, "Beside that, for matter to exist, there must be a creator of matter and a source of all its energy."[2]

Third, the **teleological** argument states that every design must have a designer.

> What shall we say, then, of our visible universe, the heavens and the earth, which are of still more remarkable structure [than Angkor Wat or the Taj Mahal] and of far more complicated design and permanence? Unavoidably all this called for the existence and activity of a personal intelligence with abil-

ity and a life-span boundlessly greater than those of intelligent man.[3]

Fourth, the **anthropological** argument—that man is an intelligent being; therefore, there must be an intelligent Being Who made him thus—is alluded to, though not pressed to its fullest: "Look at man himself! In what a wonderful, yes, fear-inspiring way he is constructed!"[4]

In addition to the four standard arguments for God's existence, an argument from history is also used:

God lives, and we can know it and we do know it because he is a historical God. He is a history-making God. From the very beginning he has intervened in human affairs, and, happily, he is intervening in human affairs today.[5]

From these arguments, we can see that the Witnesses agree that God exists and has always existed.

God's Nature

In dealing with the nature of God, the Witnesses are orthodox on His spirituality but not on His personality, unity or Trinity. Let us examine Witness teaching in each of these four areas of theology proper.

The Spirituality of God. The Jehovah's Witnesses teach the spirituality of God, that is, that God is a spirit. *Let God Be True* points this out: "His first creatures were spirit creatures, spirit like himself. Jesus said: 'God is a Spirit, and those worshipping him must worship with spirit and truth' (John 4:24, NWT)."[6] Again it is stated that He is an "incorruptible Spirit Person, with senses

of sight, hearing, and so forth."[7] In the Witnesses'
eyes, Jehovah is, in fact, the Great Spirit.

As a spirit He is incorruptible and invisible:
"Because he is a spirit, Jehovah is and will ever
be invisible to human eyes."[8] Since He is a spirit,
He is also immaterial.[9] We can see from the Witnesses' own writings, then, that they are orthodox
on the spirituality of God.

The Personality of God. The Watchtower Society teaches that God is a Person. He is "the Great
Spirit, the great intelligent active Personage invisible to man."[10] He is the "greatest Personality in
the universe, distinguished by that exclusive
name, the Great Theocrat, the Unfailing Purposer,
the True and Living God, Creator and Supreme
Sovereign of the universe."[11]

It should be noted, however, that while God
is a Person, "according to Jehovah's Witnesses,
the only true God, in one person, is Jehovah."[12]
While Christ is held to be a person, He is not the
Second Person of the Godhead. The Spirit, on the
other hand, is not considered to be a person at all,
much less the Third Person of the Godhead. "That
the Lord God Almighty seated on the throne is just
one Person, not three, Revelation 4:9 to 5:13 pro-
ceeds to show,"[13] according to Witness interpretation.

The Unity of God. The unity of God means
His oneness of essence or substance and being,
as the one and only Deity. To the Witnesses, however, it means that He is possessed of a single personality, as we discussed above. The book *Things
in Which It Is Impossible for God to Lie* devotes
fifteen pages to an attempt to prove that God is
a single unity.[14] According to Witness theology,

Christ cannot possess oneness of essence with the
Father, for Christ is a creature while God is the
Creator. Neither is Christ one in substance, for
"Jesus [is] not equal to the Father in power and
glory, but subject to Him."[15] Christ is not one with
God the Father in being, for whereas God is eter-
nal, "The truth of the matter is that the Word is
God's Son who became Jesus Christ and who did
have a beginning."[16]

You may ask, "What about Jesus' own words
in John 10:30 where Jesus plainly stated, 'I and my
Father are one'?" This is no problem to the Witnesses, given their system of interpretation. It
turns out that Christ is simply one with the Father
"in agreement, purpose and organization."[17]

Moreover, the Holy Spirit does not possess
oneness of essence or being with the Father
either, for the Spirit is not a person at all according
to the Witnesses. He is simply "the invisible active
force of Almighty God which moves his servants
to do his will."[18]

The Trinity of God. The doctrine of the Trinity of God means that although God is one in being and substance, yet He possesses three personal distinctions which are revealed to us as Father,
Son and Holy Spirit. In other words, He is one in
essence but three in Person. The Father is God,
the Son is God and the Holy Spirit is God. These
three are one God.

As could be expected, the doctrine of the
Trinity is fiercely attacked in Watchtower literature. This rejection of the Trinity goes back to
Russell, who said it was of pagan origin. His explanation is, "Nimrod married his mother, Semir-
amis, so that in a sense he was his own father, and

his own son. Here was the origin of the Trinity doctrine."[19] It appears that Russell not only tampered with theology, he also tampered with history. Nonetheless, Russell's view of the Trinity has continued to be the view of the Witnesses. The book *Let God Be True* states, "The origin of the trinity doctrine is traced back to the ancient Babylonians and Egyptians and other ancient mythologists."[20]

The doctrine of the Trinity is also attributed to the devil: "The obvious conclusion is, therefore, that Satan is the originator of the trinity doctrine."[21] Likewise, the doctrine of the Trinity is caricatured to make it appear ridiculous:

> Some will try to illustrate it by using triangles, trefoils, or images with three heads on one neck. Nevertheless, sincere persons who want to know the true God and serve him find it a bit difficult to love and worship a complicated, freakish-looking three-headed God. The clergy who inject such ideas will contradict themselves in the very next breath by stating that God made man in his own image; for certainly no one has ever seen a three-headed human creature.[22]

Such reasoning is ludicrous. No Bible-believing pastor ever preaches that God is three-headed! Furthermore, the Bible's statement that God made man in His own image (Gen. 1:27) refers to the fact that man, like God, is an intellectual and moral being. It does not mean that man is made in the physical image of God, for God is a Spirit.

Here is another Witness argument against the Trinity:

Yes, it would be a mystery if the trinity doctrine were true. One of the most mysterious things is the question, Who ran the universe during the three days that Jesus was dead and in the grave, or for that matter, during his thirty-three and a half years on earth while he was made a "little lower than the angels"? If Jesus was God, then during Jesus' death God was dead and in the grave. What a wonderful opportunity for Satan to take complete control![23]

Again the argument is absurd. God the Father and God the Holy Spirit ran the universe during the three days that Jesus was dead and in the grave. This is no problem at all, for God is one in essence but three in Person. Besides, death does not mean extinction but separation. Jesus did not become extinct! At death His spirit separated from His body. His spirit went to be with the Father, as Luke 23:46 makes clear, and His body was taken to the grave, as Luke 23:52-55 makes just as clear. Incidentally, this same portion of Scripture shows that the Witness doctrine of annihilation at death is wholly unscriptural.

Furthermore, in seeking to discredit the doctrine of the Trinity, the Witnesses point out that while the Catholic church, the largest religious body in the world, believes in the Trinity, "the religious organization ranking next in numbers (445,949,000 in the year 1965) is the Islamic or Mohammedan. They reject the 'Trinity'."[24] However, this is a senseless form of reasoning, for Moslems, Jews *and* Catholics would reject most Witness doctrines. By this reasoning all these doctrines must be false.

Again the Trinity is denied because the word "trinity" occurs nowhere in the Scriptures. Much is made of this point.[25] However, neither does the word *theocracy* appear in Scripture. Yet the concept of theocracy is held very firmly by the Witnesses. Another objection raised is that, according to the Watchtower, Jesus, the apostles and the early Christians they taught did not believe in a Trinity. Yet no Witness has ever been able to turn to even *one* verse where Jesus or the apostles denied the Trinity. This is simply an argument from silence.

What about the Bible passages that teach the Trinity? The Witnesses deal with these passages in a rather superficial manner. For example, such a clear passage as John 1:1—"the Word was God"—is passed off with the comment that it only mentions two Persons, not three:

> What about the statement at John 1:1 (AV) which refers to Jesus as "the Word," saying: "In the beginning was the Word, and the Word was with God, and the Word was God"? Does that not prove the "Trinity"? No. Notice first of all, that only two persons are mentioned, not three.[26]

This argument is so weak that in the New World Translation the Witnesses sought to take care of the problem once and for all by translating John 1:1 as "The Word was a god." They would not change their theology to fit the Bible so they changed the Bible to fit their theology!

But suppose we turn to passages that mention all three Persons of the Godhead, such as at the baptism of *Christ* when the *Spirit* came as a dove, and the *Father* spoke in a voice from Heaven (Mark 1:9–11)—would that convince the Witnesses? No, for here another tactic is used. Instead of accepting these passages because all three are mentioned, the Witnesses argue, "Scriptures mentioning Father, Son and Holy Spirit together do not say they are equal, coeternal or one God."[27] The obvious answer to this argument is that the Scriptures do not use those exact terms because the Bible was not written as a systematic theology.

Since the Witnesses reject the Trinity, they actually have two Gods and fall into the error of bitheism. On the one hand, Jehovah is Almighty God. On the other hand, "Jesus Christ is a God, but not the Almighty God."[28] Again Jesus is "referred to as a Mighty God, but not the Almighty God, Jehovah."[29] Thus, to the Witnesses, Jesus Christ and His Father are not one God but are separate and distinct Gods.

God's Attributes

What is God like? To answer that question, one must look at the attributes—that is, the characteristics or qualities—of God. The attributes of God may be divided into two classes: His natural attributes, i. e., those that pertain to His existence as an infinite, rational Spirit; and His moral attributes, i. e., those that belong to Him as a righteous or moral Spirit.

Let us first study His natural attributes. On some of these the Witnesses are orthodox; on others, such as God's omnipresence, they are unorthodox.

The Omniscience of God. The word "omniscience" comes from two Latin words meaning "all" and "knowledge"—thus, God is all-knowing. The Witnesses seem to be orthodox on the omniscience of God the Father. Such statements as "[The] creative works are evidence of the existence of [an] intelligent God"[30] allude to this doctrine, although they do not directly state it. However, Gruss plainly states the Witness belief in the attribute: "God is omniscient."[31]

Christ evidently does not share in this omniscience. Much is made of Christ's statement in Matthew 24:36 and Mark 13:32 pertaining to His coming: "When Jesus was on earth he certainly was *not* equal to his Father; for he said there were some things that neither he nor the angels knew but that only God knew."[32] What the Witnesses fail to realize is that this "lack of knowledge" was due to Christ's *kenosis,* His voluntary setting aside of some of His attributes some of the time while He was here on earth. This great truth is taught in Philippians 2:6–8.

The Omnipotence of God. The word "omnipotence" again comes from the Latin, *omnis* and *potens,* meaning "all" and "power." By this attribute it is meant that God has unlimited power. As can be expected, the Witnesses hold that this is one of His principal attributes.[33] "He is the Almighty and Supreme One."[34] "His power and knowledge extend everywhere."[35] God's power is exercised in light of His other attributes. He uses it with a right purpose and for the good of those who love that which is right.

This omnipotence is limited solely to God the Father, according to the Witnesses. Christ does not share this attribute. He is a mighty God, but He is not almighty. According to the Watchtower interpretation, the Bible does not say that the Son is equal to the Father in power: How could Jesus "be 'equal in power and glory' with the heavenly Father? He could not be such, nor does the Holy Bible say this."[36]

It follows, of course, that the Witnesses believe that the Holy Spirit is not omnipotent since He is not a person. He relates to this attribute in that He is the invisible force of Almighty God, according to the Watchtower, and He is the means by which God exercises His omnipotence.

The Omnipresence of God. Omnipresence is that attribute of God whereby He is present everywhere. Surprisingly, the Witnesses do not believe that God possesses this attribute, although they believe He is omniscient and omnipotent. He is "not omnipresent, but can project spirit anywhere to accomplish His purpose."[37] "Although Jehovah is the almighty and supreme sovereign of the universe, he is not omnipresent ... his presence is limited to heaven, from which his power reaches everywhere."[38] Needless to say, Christ does not possess this attribute either, according to the Watchtower.

Nonetheless, the writer of Psalm 139, King David, certainly believed in the omnipresence of God. He wrote: "Whither shall I go from thy spirit? or whither shall I flee from thy presence? If I ascend up into heaven, thou art there: if I make my bed in hell, behold, thou art there" (Ps. 139:7, 8). The apostle Paul taught the same truth, "In him we live, and move, and have our being ..." (Acts 17:28).

The Eternality of God. The eternality of God refers to the fact that God is of infinite duration, having no beginning or end. He always was, is and always will be. The Watchtower teaches the eternality of God the Father: "He is God and, as such, never had a beginning. His eternalness is declared also at Isaiah 57:15: 'Thus saith the high and lofty One that inhabiteth eternity, whose name is Holy; I dwell in the high and holy place.' "[39] Again it is stated, "As the Creator of all things, Jehovah God, the 'King of eternity,' existed before all others. He is 'from everlasting to everlasting,' meaning that he had no beginning and will never have an end."[40]

The attribute of eternality is not extended to Christ. "Only Jehovah is from everlasting to everlasting."[41] Jesus, according to the Watchtower, is a created being and had a beginning: The "Son of God had a beginning, was created."[42]

The Immutability of God. The attribute of immutability means that God does not change as far as His nature, attributes and counsels are concerned. These are absolutely perfect, and therefore there can be no variation in them. Witness theology agrees that God is immutable[43] and correspondingly teaches that ". . . he is self-contained, which means he is complete in himself and lacks nothing."[44]

This attribute is not extended to Christ. According to the Witnesses, before Christ's incarnation He was a spirit being; while on earth He was a human being; now He is the angel Michael.[45] Orthodox theology teaches that eternally Christ was God; on earth He became also a man, having the two natures in one Person. As God, He was, is and always will be immutable.

We have examined the natural attributes of

God—omniscience, omnipotence, omnipresence, eternality and immutability. Let us now examine what the Witnesses teach concerning God's moral attributes.

The Holiness and Righteousness of God. The attribute of holiness means on the one hand that God is entirely apart from all that is evil and on the other hand that God has perfect purity and absolute integrity of nature and character. Righteousness refers to that characteristic of God that always leads Him to do right and to demand that which is right. Truthfulness is another attribute closely related to holiness. In Witness theology all of these attributes are held to be true of God the Father.[46]

The Witnesses also hold that holiness is attributed to Christ. However, they say, Christ was sinless as a perfect Man, not as a Person of the Godhead. They also add that by Jesus' maintaining integrity as a perfect Human, He proved that it was not impossible for Adam to have done so.

The Justice of God. The justice of God is that attribute that always leads Him to be just and to demand that which is just. The Witnesses believe in this attribute of God. "Jehovah, therefore, is not an oppressive God. 'All his ways are justice' (Deuteronomy 32:4)."[47]

God's justice, so say the Witnesses, precludes Christ's deity. "God's justice would not let Jesus, as a ransom, be more than a perfect man. So he could not be the supreme God Almighty in the flesh."[48] It seems strange to use an attribute of the Father to deny one of the Son!

The Wisdom of God. The Witnesses believe that wisdom is one of the principal attributes of

Jehovah. "With Jehovah there are 'wisdom and mightiness; he has counsel and understanding' (Job 12:13). Evidence of his wisdom is seen in all his creative works, in both heaven and earth."[49]

The Love of God. The Watchtower agrees that God is a God of love and compassion. "We can be happy indeed to have such a just yet compassionate God as our Supreme Judge, Lawgiver, and King."[50] "It is because of God's long-suffering that we have had opportunity to live at all."[51] Although love is viewed as one of the principal attributes of God, it is subordinate to His vindication, which lays stress on His power and justice. "Because of his great love for mankind, God will bring an end to wickedness."[52]

As touching the attributes of God, then, the Witnesses are usually orthodox in regard to God the Father but unorthodox in regard to God the Son and God the Holy Spirit.

The Person and Work of the Father

Not much needs to be said regarding the Witness view of the Person of the Father except to comment on their view of God as the Father of Jesus Christ. Here the Witnesses are most unorthodox. God is said to be the Father of Christ in that He created Christ. Christ is the "First Creation by God."[53] Thus the eternal generation of Christ is denied. God is also said to be the Father of the angels in that they are likewise created beings. This is indirect Fatherhood, however, since it is held that angels were created by Christ, who was in turn created by God the Father.[54]

The work of the Father as stressed by the Watchtower concerns creation, preservation and the theocracy. Creation took place billions of years ago, and since then God has been at work preserving it: "He has not only created but also responsibly held this universe together throughout its billions of years of existence."[55] Jehovah was the only Creator; Christ, nonetheless, as the first creation was used as a master worker in creating all other things.[56] It was this view that forced the Watchtower to add the word "other" to the New World text of Colossians 1:16 and 17 no less than four times (see page 56).

The angels were created before the earth.[57] The length of the days of creation were not twenty-four hours but "about 7,000 years" each.[58] Jehovah created Adam and Eve in 4026 B.C. and placed them in the Garden of Eden, which was in the area now called Armenia. The first pair spoke Hebrew.[59]

The vindication of Jehovah's name is one of the major works of God. "His vindication is more important than the salvation of men."[60] Thus Christ came primarily to vindicate the name of Jehovah and only secondarily to pay a ransom for men.[61]

Another of the works of the Father is His theocracy, or rule, over men. The idea of the theocracy is the foundation of Witness theology.[62] It is also the inducement to keep the Witnesses working. This rule, of course, is at present centering around the work of the Watchtower, the only organization that can rightfully be called "God's organization," as the Witnesses are constantly reminded. Eventually the theocracy will be realized worldwide after the battle of Armageddon takes place.

"It is characteristic of all false cults to deny the Deity of Christ and the JW's are certainly no exception to this infamous rule."
F. W. Thomas,
Masters of Deception, p. 11

"Prior to coming to earth, this only-begotten Son of God did not think himself to be co-equal with Jehovah God."
Let God Be True, Rev. ed., p. 34

7

THE SON DOES NOT SHINE

THE apostle Paul clearly defines the gospel in the epistle of 1 Corinthians, "Moreover, brethren, I declare unto you the gospel . . . how that Christ died for our sins according to the scriptures; And that he was buried, and that he rose again the third day according to the scriptures" (1 Cor. 15:1, 3, 4). The Person and work of Christ is the very core of true Christianity, making the doctrine of Christology of utmost importance. What do the Witnesses teach concerning Christology? Let us examine their teachings concerning His preexistence, His virgin birth, His Person and His work.

Christ's Preexistence

The Watchtower teaches that Christ was preexistent, although He was not deity. "Rather, before coming to earth He was the first created being, the archangel Michael, the chief representative of God."[1] Thus, before being born to Mary in Bethlehem, Jesus was an angel. So God sent the angel Gabriel to Mary (Luke 1:26, 27) to tell her that she would bear a son; and this son was another angel. At that point He ceased to be an angel and became a human being.

Moreover, according to the Watchtower, although Jesus was preexistent, He was not eternally so. He had a beginning, getting His start when God began His creative work. Prior to that time Jehovah was completely alone. Since Christ was previously Michael, the archangel, He did not differ from the other angels in kind, only in degree. He was superior because He was the first one created and He helped God create the rest. In this prehuman state He did not possess immortality. Later God gave Him the opportunity to gain it.

However, the Bible teaches that Christ was preexistent not as an angel, but as God.

> Micah 5:2 teaches the eternity of the Son, for the word translated "from of old" is used in Habakkuk 1:12 of God's eternal nature; thus what God is, the Son is (see also Is. 9:6). Furthermore, He Himself claimed to be preexistent, for He said, "Before Abraham [came to be], I am" (Jn. 8:58). The statement, "I am," is not only a claim to existence before Abraham but also is a reference to the sacred name of God, *Yahweh*, and thus a claim to be God (Ex. 3:14–15).[2]

Christ's Virgin Birth

While liberal theologians deny the virgin birth of Christ, this is one doctrine the Witnesses affirm concerning Christ:

To become born of Mary the heavenly Son had to lay aside all his heavenly glory and position. At God's due time for his only-begotten Son to become a man, Jehovah took the perfect life of his only-begotten Son and transferred it from heaven to the egg cell in the womb of the unmarried girl Mary. God, by his almighty power, was able to take the personality of his only-begotten Son, his life pattern, and put this personality within the powers of the tiny bundle of live energy that he placed into the womb of Mary.[3]

In another place, this same Witness book plainly states the Virgin Birth: "Mary was a virgin."[4]

The date of Christ's birth in Bethlehem was "about the first of October, in the year 2 B.C."[5] Although the Witnesses believe in the Virgin Birth, one should not think that they believe in the incarnation of Christ. They do not.[6] They say that Christ was not God clothed in flesh. In fact, when He was born, He even ceased to be Michael, the archangel. He was no longer a spirit being of any kind. He was now a human being, nothing more. He was not clothed in flesh, He was flesh.

Since Jesus was now human and not angel at all and did not have two natures, the Witness teaching of the preexistence of Christ is completely undermined. Hoekema rightly points this out:

> Since previous to his birth from Mary, the Son of God is said to have had a spirit nature, of which he divested himself at the time he came to earth, we must conclude, according

to Watchtower teaching, that the Christ who was born in Bethlehem is not the same individual who existed previously as the Archangel Michael.[7]

Christ's Person

Orthodox Christianity teaches that Christ is both God and Man, that He has two natures in one Person. The Witnesses violently deny the deity of Christ: "Jesus is the Son of God, not God the Son."[8] Let us now examine Witness teachings concerning the deity and the humanity of Jesus Christ.

The Deity of Christ. It is true that the Witnesses say that Jesus was "a god." The New World Translation renders John 1:1 as "Originally the Word was, and the Word was with God, and the Word was a god."[9] They even go so far as to say that Christ was a mighty God, using the capital "G." However, Christ was not the Almighty God, neither, according to the Watchtower, did He share in the nature or essence of God the Father.

Although they admit that Jesus was the only-begotten Son of God, the Witnesses hold that He nonetheless was still a creature. He can be called "only begotten" even though He was one angel out of millions of angels, because He was the first and helped God create the rest. The Witnesses seek to refute the belief that Christ was not a creature in the following manner:

> Well, then, was there some female person in heaven by whom Jehovah God *begot* his only-begotten Son? If there were, then that female person would have to be before the only-begotten Son of God. But the Holy Bible does not teach such a thing. Rather, the only-

begotten Son was the original and first direct creation by God without any intermediary such as a wife or female person. Also, because of begetting, we are not to imagine that God has a womb like a female person. God is not female.[10]

Such an argument is ludicrous to say the least. Not one orthodox, Bible-believing theologian would say God had a female partner and in that sense begat Christ! But for those who follow the Watchtower line of reasoning, this argument proves Christ is not of the same essence as God the Father.

Witnesses teach that Christ is not the God-Man, that He is inferior to Jehovah. He was less than God in His prehuman state, in His human state and in His "posthuman" state. "Prior to coming to earth, this only-begotten Son of God did not think himself to be coequal with Jehovah God."[11]

At the time of His baptism, Christ in some way again became God's spirit Son. "By acknowledging him as his beloved Son, God begot Jesus to be his spiritual Son once more instead of a human Son."[12] So Jesus was twice begotten by God! Moreover, at that time He became the Messiah— He was not the Messiah from birth.

The Biblical View of the Deity of Christ. Although the Watchtower loudly denies Christ's deity, the Bible shows His deity in at least a half a dozen ways.

Divine names. First, in Hebrews 1:8 Christ is called *God*: "But unto the Son he saith, Thy throne, *O God*, is for ever and ever: a sceptre of righteousness is the sceptre of thy kingdom"

(KJV). The very literal New American Standard Bible has the same: "But of the Son He says, Thy throne, *O God,* is forever and ever." And the New International Version: "But about the Son he says, 'Your throne, *O God,* will last for ever and ever.' "

The New World Translation grossly mistranslates this verse to make it fit Witness theology: "But with reference to the Son: 'God is your throne forever.' " This translation is ludicrous. Revelation 3:21 tells us that we will join Christ when He sits on His throne (the NWT also says this). Christ will not sit on God, and neither will we!

The Greek text clearly shows that Hebrews 1:8 is a statement of the deity of Christ. "Pros de ton uion, O thronos sou, *o theos,* eis ton aiona tou aionos." This verse calls Christ *theos*—God. It could not be any clearer. Our word *theology*—the study of God—comes from this word.

Second, Christ is called *Lord.* In Acts 9:17 Christ is referred to as "the Lord." The verse leaves no doubt that it is speaking of Christ, for it goes on to say, "even Jesus." The New World Translation also says in this verse that Christ is the Lord. "Saul, brother, the Lord, the Jesus that appeared to you on the road over which you were coming, has sent me forth." The Greek word for Lord here is *kurios.*

In John 13:13 Jesus says, "You address me, 'Teacher,' and '*Lord,*' and you speak rightly, for I am such" (NWT). The word again is *kurios.*

Now let us see what the New World Translation has for Revelation 1:8. " 'I am the Alpha and the Omega,' says Jehovah God, 'the One who is and who was and who is coming, the Almighty.' "

The one speaking is *Jehovah*. Next, go to the Greek and what word do we find for Jehovah? *Kurios!* Thus Jesus *is* Jehovah God. Sincere persons who want to know the truth of God's own Word can check the Greek for themselves.

Divine worship. The Bible teaches us that we should worship only God. The New World Translation translates Matthew 4:10 thus: " 'It is Jehovah your God you must worship, and it is to him alone you must render sacred service.' "

Revelation 22:8 and 9 support this and further tell us that we are forbidden to worship angels: "Well, I John was the one hearing and seeing these things. And when I had heard and seen, I fell down to worship before the feet of the angel that had been showing me these things. But he tells me: 'Be careful! Do not do that! All I am is a fellow slave of you and of your brothers who are prophets and of those who are observing the words of this scroll. Worship God' " (NWT). Acts 10:25 and 26 take us one step further. We are not to worship man. The apostle Peter forbids such an action. So we are not to worship either angels or man, but only God.

Because Jesus is God, the disciples worshiped Him. "And as they went to tell his disciples, behold, Jesus met them, saying, All hail. And they came and held him by the feet, and worshiped him" (Matt. 28:9). If He were simply a man, or an angel, He would not have accepted worship.

Divine offices. Moreover, Jesus has divine offices. First, He is the Creator. "All things came into existence through him, and apart from him not even one thing came into existence" (John 1:3, NWT). Second, Christ is the Preserver of all things:

"He sustains all things by the word of his power" (Heb. 1:3b, NWT). Third, He is the One Who alone can forgive sins: "the Son of man has authority to forgive sins upon the earth" (Mark 2:10, NWT).

Divine attributes. Christ's deity can also be seen in His divine attributes. He has all authority (Matt. 28:18); He has divine omniscience (Mark 2:8; John 2:24) and He has divine omnipresence (Matt. 18:20).

A Final Word. Jesus is acknowledged to be God. Let the New World Translation speak for itself. First, at the time of His birth: " 'Look! The virgin will become pregnant and will give birth to a son, and they will call his name Immanuel' which means, when translated, 'With Us Is God' " (Matt. 1:23, NWT). Second, just after His resurrection, Christ came to the room where the disciples were and greeted them. "Next he said to Thomas: 'Put your finger here, and see my hands, and take your hand and stick it into my side, and stop being unbelieving but become believing.' In answer Thomas said to him, 'my Lord and my God!' " (John 20:28, NWT).

The Humanity of Christ. The Witnesses believe in the humanity of Christ. Unlike the Gnostics of old or Christian Scientists of today, they believe this was a real humanity. Not only do they believe that Jesus was really human, they teach that He was a perfect human. "Having a perfect Father as his life source, Jesus did not inherit imperfection from his imperfect mother Mary."[13] However, although Jesus was a perfect human, according to the Watchtower, He was only a perfect man. He did not possess two natures in one person; He possessed only one nature.

The Witnesses argue that if He had been more than a perfect human He could not have served as a ransom for sinful man.

Christ's Work

In examining the work of Christ as it is found in Watchtower literature, six subtopics come to our attention: Christ's work in vindicating Jehovah; His work in paying a ransom for man; His resurrection from the dead; His ascension up into Heaven; His present ministry during this age; and His coming back to earth again. Let us investigate these in this order.

The Vindication of Jehovah. The primary purpose of Christ's coming to earth, says the Watchtower, was to vindicate Jehovah. His coming in order to provide salvation for man was only secondary.[14] The way Christ vindicated Jehovah was by proving that a perfect man could live for God and remain faithful to Him in spite of whatever Satan did. "By Jesus' maintaining integrity as a perfect human he proved that it was not impossible for Adam to have done so."[15] Thus Satan, who got Adam to fall and who thought he could make every man sin, was shown to be false, and Jehovah was vindicated. In other words, it proved that Jehovah *could* make a man Satan could not seduce.

The Atonement or Ransom by Christ. The Witness view of the atonement centers on the ransom that Christ made. However, the atonement could not be an infinite God paying an infinite price for the sins of the world because Jesus was not God. "Has your church told you that Jesus is Almighty God? If so, it has not told you the truth."[16] Rather, the Watchtower says, the ransom by Christ was that of a perfect man.

The need for a ransom existed because the first man, Adam, transgressed God's law. Thereby "he forfeited perfect human life with its rights and prospects."[17] He then became imperfect and fathered a race of imperfect men. "Adam lost perfect human life. Hence, the ransom price for the human race would have to be a perfect human life. Only a perfect human life could balance the scale of perfect justice."[18] None of Adam's descendants could provide such a price for himself or for any other person.

Although Christ was virgin born, He did not inherit imperfection from His mother, Mary. Christ's life principle was transferred by God to the womb of Mary. "This made it possible for His Son, Jesus, to be born 'holy,' without sin."[19] As the perfect Son of God, Christ could then lay down His perfect human life in sacrifice, thus furnishing the valuable price required to ransom the human race.

Christ died on a "torture stake." The Witnesses never use the word "cross," except in derision. Christ accepted the penalty that was intended for sinful man. On the basis of His ransom, Jehovah can declare humans righteous. It was Christ's perfect life for man's imperfect one. "As a perfect man, Jesus stood in a position similar to that once occupied by the perfect man Adam, a righteous, perfect, sinless human."[20] In reality, then, Christ was nothing more than Adam once was. He certainly does not fare too well in Watchtower theology.

A question the Witnesses fail to answer is how

one perfect human life (not an infinite one) could be an exact, corresponding ransom for not just one imperfect life but for *many* imperfect lives— for untold millions.

The Resurrection of Christ. Romans 4:25 states that Christ "was raised again for our justification." His resurrection was part of His work. Although the Witnesses say that Christ arose, they do not mean a bodily resurrection such as orthodox Christianity teaches. They believe He rose as a spirit being. This teaching is not new among the followers of this movement, for it goes back to Russell himself. In 1889 Russell wrote:

> Our Lord's human body, however, was supernaturally removed from the tomb . . . . We know nothing about what became of it except that it did not decay or corrupt (Acts 2:27, 31). Whether it was dissolved into gases, or whether it is still preserved somewhere as the grand memorial of God's love, of Christ's obedience, and our redemption, no one knows.[21]

This view of a nonphysical resurrection was perpetuated by Rutherford, who surmised that Jehovah may have preserved Christ's body somewhere in order to exhibit it to the people living in the millennial age.[22] The book entitled *The Truth Shall Make You Free*, published early in the reign of Knorr, carries on this false teaching.[23]

At the time of this "resurrection," He ceased to be a human and again became a spirit, a perfect spiritual being of the highest order. This teaching that Christ rose from the dead but that His body did not come back to life has caused some to argue that the Witnesses do not believe in the resurrection of Christ.[24] Yet the Witnesses say, "The resurrection of Jesus is no illusion or imagined thing."[25]

The Witnesses believe that on the third day after His death, Christ was raised from the grave by God, not as a human being, but as a spirit and was granted immortality as the angel Michael. Since His body is still dead, it amounts to a resurrection without a resurrection!

If the question were asked, "What about the appearances of Christ after His resurrection? Do not those prove He rose bodily from the grave?" the answer is that they were materializations: "For forty days after that he materialized, as angels before him had done, to show himself alive to his disciples as witnesses."[26] The Witnesses go on to say that the bodies He took on were not always the same.

However, if this were true, Jesus was not the "perfect being" the Witnesses say He was, for He deceived Thomas into thinking that His body had come back to life when He said, ". . . Reach hither thy finger, and behold my hands; and reach hither thy hand, and thrust it into my side: and be not faithless, but believing" (John 20:27). If Christ were a deceiver, He was no better than Adam and therefore could be a ransom for no one. It is only logical, then, to believe what the Bible teaches—that Christ rose physically from the dead.

The Ascension of Christ. The Witnesses believe that Christ ascended into Heaven but that He ascended as a spirit creature. His ascension was not a bodily one. They argue that if Jesus had taken His human body to Heaven, He could not have become ruler over the angels, for He would have remained a little lower than them. "God did not purpose for Jesus to be humiliated thus forever by being a fleshly man forever."[27]

They also teach that if Christ had risen physically from the dead and ascended physically into Heaven, the ransom paid would have been nullified, for He would be taking back what He laid down. The error here is that the Witnesses view the ransom as the work of a perfect human forfeiting humanity. However, the Bible teaches that Christ has redeemed us by bearing our sins on the cross: "Who his own self bare our sins in his own body on the tree, that we, being dead to sins, should live unto righteousness: by whose stripes ye were healed" (1 Pet. 2:24).

The Present Ministry of Christ. The Watchtower teaches that after Christ sacrificed His perfect manhood and God raised Him to deathless life as an immortal spirit being, God exalted Him above all other angels: "Now Jesus is made the Head under Jehovah of God's capital organization over the entire universe."[28] This statement should not be taken to mean that the Son is equal with the Father since, as we have noted, the Son does not shine in Witness theology: "God the Father did not exalt the Son to be His equal, but graciously gave him the second-highest place in all the realm of life."[29]

Jesus became King of the New World Society in 1914. Even so, He is still subject to Jehovah. Furthermore, according to the Witnesses, Jesus, as Michael the archangel, cast Satan out of Heaven sometime between 1914 and 1918.

The Second Coming of Christ. More will be

said about the second coming of Christ under the topic of eschatology, or end-time events. Briefly, the Witnesses do not believe in a visible second coming of Christ. Instead they teach a "second presence" of Christ. Russell got this meaning of *parousia* ("second coming") from the Christadelphian, Benjamin Wilson, through Wilson's *Diaglott* translation of the New Testament.[30]

It is difficult to say how much other influence the Christadelphians had on Russell. There are striking similarities between the two:

> Actually the theological system closest to the present Watchtower is that of a tiny and curious sect known as the Christadelphians. They number no more than 15,000 members. Like Jehovah's Witnesses, they are both unitarian and adventist. They too reject the Trinity and the divinity of Jesus Christ. Only the righteous will win eternal life while the wicked are doomed to suffer annihilation. The Second Coming is imminent.[31]

Taking *parousia* to mean "presence" instead of "coming," Russell affirmed that it took place in 1874. At that time Christ returned to the upper air. Four years later, in the spring of 1878, the twelve apostles and the dead members of the little flock were raised to meet the Lord in the air and then began floating about in the air. Current Witnesses place Christ's second "coming" in 1914.

A Parting Word

The Witnesses have a low view of Christ. They deny His deity, His bodily resurrection from the dead, His physical ascension to Heaven and His visible second coming in glory. This view of

Christ is also reflected in the dating method used by the Watchtower. Instead of using B.C. (before Christ) and A.D. (*anno Domini*, i.e., the year of our Lord), they now use B.C.E (before the common era) and C.E. (the common era).[32] This is just one more example of the Witness shift away from the centrality of Christ to all of life.

"Quench not the Spirit."
1 Thessalonians 5:19

"Undoubtedly, the least under-
stood person of the Godhead is the
Holy Spirit."

Charles C. Ryrie,
A Survey of Bible Doctrine, p. 67

8

QUENCHING THE SPIRIT

AS we approach the area of pneumatology, or the doctrine of the Holy Spirit, we come to another crucial point in Biblical theology. A proper understanding of the Person and work of the Holy Spirit is basic to all other areas of doctrine. After all, Jesus Christ Himself stated that the Spirit would guide us into all truth (John 16:13).

It is at this point that we face a major obstacle in Witness theology, for in its views on pneumatology the Witness movement is so unorthodox that it really is not possible to discuss the *Person* and *work* of the Spirit. Nevertheless, for the sake of a systematic theological treatment of the subject, these categories will still be used.

The Person of the Spirit

Orthodox Christianity teaches that the Holy Spirit is a Person, indeed, the Third Person of the Trinity. Jehovah's Witnesses deny this outright: "As for the holy spirit with which Jesus was anointed, this spirit is not a person at all but is God's invisible active force by means of which God carries out his holy will and work."[1]

Another argument of the Witnesses against the personality of the Spirit has to do with the testimony of John the Baptist concerning the baptism of Jesus. "John the Baptist said that Jesus would baptize with holy spirit even as John had been baptizing with water. Water is not a person nor is holy spirit a person."[2] This argument is meaningless. Water is a liquid. By this reasoning the Witnesses should hold that the Spirit is a liquid too!

Notice in the above quotation that the words "holy spirit" are not capitalized. This is standard practice in the New World Translation. Likewise it will be noticed that there is no article before "holy spirit." This is also found many times in the New World Translation. ". . . And they all became filled with holy spirit" (Acts 2:4); ". . . but YOU will be baptized in holy spirit not many days after this" (Acts 1:5). These are indirect methods of teaching that the Holy Spirit is not a Person.

According to the Witnesses, heavenly visions of God and His Son reveal no personal Holy Spirit. It is also said that the masculine pronoun referring to the Spirit does not show personality. However, Greek grammar proves this to be wrong:

> The Greek word for spirit is *pneuma* (from which we derive words that have to do with air, like *pneumatic* or *pneumonia*), and it is a neuter gender word. Proper grammar teaches us that when a pronoun is substituted for a noun it must be of the same gender as the noun, but this is not always the

case when pronouns are substituted for the word *Spirit.* In John 16:13-14, for instance, the pronoun "he" ("howbeit when he" and "he shall glorify me") is masculine. . . . These are not instances of bad grammar but excellent theology, for they show that the Spirit is not a neuter thing but a definite person.[3]

Furthermore, the Bible shows that the Holy Spirit possesses the attributes of personality—intellect, emotion and will. First, He has intellect. Romans 8:27 speaks of "the mind of the Spirit," and 1 Corinthians 2:10 and 11 state that the Spirit knows the things of God. Second, the Spirit has emotion. Ephesians 4:30 shows that it is possible to grieve the Spirit; thus, He must be a Person. It certainly is not possible to grieve a force. Third, the Spirit has a will. First Corinthians 12:11 states that the Spirit distributes spiritual gifts "as he wills." A person has a will. A force does not. Since the Spirit has all three attributes of a person—intellect, emotion and will—He certainly must be a Person.

Moreover, the Holy Spirit performs the actions of a person:

He teaches: "He shall teach you all things, and bring all things to your remembrance" (John 14:26; see also 1 Cor. 2:13).

He testifies: "He shall testify of me" (John 15:26).

He guides: "For as many as are led by the Spirit of God, they are the sons of God" (Rom. 8:14); "When he, the Spirit of truth, is come, he will guide you into all truth" (John 16:13).

He reproves: "He will reprove the world of sin" (John 16:8).

He speaks and commands: "Then the Spirit said unto Philip, Go near, and join thyself to this chariot" (Acts 8:29).

He performs miracles: "The Spirit of the Lord caught away Philip, that the eunuch saw him no more" (Acts 8:39).

He can be lied to: "But Peter said, Ananias, why hath Satan filled thine heart to lie to the Holy Spirit . . . thou hast not lied unto men, but unto God" (Acts 5:3, 4).

He calls for Christian service: "The Holy Ghost said, Separate me Barnabas and Saul for the work whereunto I have called them" (Acts 13:2).

Most of all, the personality of the Spirit can be seen in the fact that He prays. Only a person, not a force, can pray. The New World Translation also shows this personal action of the Spirit, ". . . the spirit itself pleads for us with groanings unuttered" (Rom. 8:26, NWT).

The Witnesses strongly assert that "Satan the Devil [is] a Person, not the mere abstract quality of evil"[4] but deny the personality of the Holy Spirit, which certainly makes one wonder about their theology.

The Work of the Spirit

Actually, we cannot speak of the work of the Spirit in Witness theology. Since, in their view, the Spirit is not a Person, He cannot carry on works. Rather, *it* is used by God to do *some* works. "*It* is God's holy active force of which he is the inexhaustible source. He gives *it* to Jesus and *it* is subject to Jesus' use and control" [italics mine].[5] "From God there goes forth an invisible active force by means of which he gets his will done."[6]

The Witnesses agree that the Spirit was used in creation. *It* was also used in the inspiration of the Bible. In old time *it* helped men do deeds of valor. *It* was used in the virgin birth of Christ. *It* serves as a radio wave to carry Christ's teaching, illumination, guidance (dynamic energy) to God's servants on earth.[7] *It* is also used to beget and anoint the ones called to the heavenly kingdom (the 144,000 elite).[8] The Jehovah's Witnesses who have been added to the movement since about 1935 are called the "other sheep" or the "great crowd." "They have never been sealed with God's spirit as an advance token of their heavenly inheritance. They have not been anointed with God's spirit as prospective joint heirs with Christ in his celestial kingdom."[9]

As far as the gifts of the Spirit are concerned, the Witnesses believe the miraculous gifts were given to the infant church, but they "are not bestowed upon the remnant today of members of Christ's body."[10] Today's church does not need them because it is full grown. Being filled with the Spirit, the church can bring forth the fruitage of the Spirit, according to Witness literature.[11]

Watchtower literature says very little about the fruit of the Spirit (Gal. 5:22, 23). The Witness book that deals mainly with the Spirit makes but four exceedingly brief references to this passage. It seems to relegate the fruit to the conditions of the new earth.[12] It is evident that the Holy Spirit is not of major importance to the Witnesses.

"And there was war in heaven:
Michael and his angels fought
against the dragon; and the dragon
fought and his angels."
Revelation 12:7

". . . that rebel spirit creature who
made a Devil out of himself. . . ."
*Did Man Get Here by Evolution or
by Creation?* p. 151

9

MICHAEL AND THE DRAGON

HAVING finished the study of the Witness doctrines concerning the Persons of the Godhead, we now move on to the two classes of personal beings created by God: angels and man. In studying the doctrine of the angels, or angelology, we are immediately made aware that there are both good and evil angels. Thus we must divide our study into two themes once more. But first, how does Christ relate to the angels?

The Relationship of Christ to the Angels

Usually the study of a religious group's teachings concerning Christ is dealt with in Christology, and the study of its teachings concerning angels is dealt with in angelology. There are two exceptions to this rule—the Jehovah's Witnesses and the Mormons. Although no two groups could be farther apart in most areas of doctrine (i.e., Witness unitarianism and Mormon polytheism), on this point they are similar. Both groups believe Christ was an angel before becoming a man.

The Witness book *Things in Which It Is Impossible for God to Lie* contains a fifteen-page chapter on angelology entitled, "When 'All the Sons of God Began Shouting in Applause.' " Nearly half of that chapter is spent on the relationship of Christ to the angels. This is because the Watchtower Society views Christ as God's first creation. "This first creation of God came to be called 'his only-begotten Son.' "[1]

When originally created, say the Witnesses, Christ was created as the angel Michael. Then He became a man. Finally, after His resurrection, He again became the angel Michael.[2] The Witnesses should logically be forbidden to worship Christ since to them He is an angel, and Colossians 2:18 indicates it is definitely wrong to worship angels.

Angelology Proper

As we begin the study of Witness teachings on angels, we will first look at angelology proper. Angelology proper covers the good angels, and it also covers the evil angels to the extent that they partake of the nature or being of the angels of God, or orginally did so.

The Origin of the Angels. The first question that comes to mind when studying the angels is, Where did they come from? The answer of the Witnesses in some ways is quite orthodox, in other ways very unorthodox. It is orthodox in that they teach that angels were created by God. It is unorthodox in the way they relate this creating of angels to Christ.

How, then, did the angels come into being according to the Watchtower? They were created by God, but only indirectly. They were created by God through Christ. The "Son [was] used as [the] Master Worker in creating all other things."[3] The Witness teaching that the angels are an indirect creation of God borders on the ancient heresy called Gnosticism with its aeons and demigods.

The time of the angels' creation is not given. However, they were created before the events of Genesis chapter one.[4]

In a sense, the Witnesses really teach that God is the "grandfather" of the angels. However, they still refer to angels as "sons of God" because their life came from Jehovah. Christ is their "older heavenly, spiritual brother."[5] This weakened view of Christ lowers Him from the realm of Creator to that of one angel among millions. The Witnesses seek to defend themselves against such an accusation by stating that He was not just an angel but the archangel, and the only one directly created by God:

> Because all these other creations were brought into existence "through him," this "first-born" Son of God remained in a unique position, forasmuch as he remained the only Son who was created or begotten directly by God the Creator. Thus he remained "only-begotten," the only direct creation of Jehovah God.[6]

Apparently the apostle Thomas was in error when he called Christ, "My Lord and my God" (John 20:28). If he had known "the truth" he would have said, "My Michael and my archangel."

The Nature of the Angels. Witness teaching concerning the nature of angels may be summarized in this statement: They are created, superior, spirit beings. First, angels are created. They are "not disembodied humans."[7] In other words, they are not human beings who had died on earth and were then transformed into heavenly spirit beings (an erroneous view held by some other cults). Second, angels are spirit beings and thus invisible. Although they are spiritual, heavenly, invisible beings, "God has given to angels power to materialize and appear in human bodies as men."[8]

Third, angels are superior to men; that is, they are on a higher plane than men intellectually, physically and spiritually. Unlike men, they do not marry or reproduce. They are numerous and fall into different classifications. Thus it may be seen that, with the glaring exception concerning Christ, the Witnesses are somewhat orthodox as to the nature of angels.

The Works of the Angels. Here again the Witnesses are quite orthodox. Angels are viewed as representatives of Jehovah and speak in His name. They are His messengers. They perform services on behalf of God's children. They protected ancient Israel. They are the executioners of divine judgment.[9]

In summary, the Witnesses are unorthodox in their angelology in the same way they are unorthodox in their Christology.

Satanology

In studying Witness theology regarding Satan, we shall follow the same three categories as given above for the good angels: origin, nature and works. In addition, it will be necessary to examine the Witness view of Satan's doom.

The Origin of Satan. "Who made Satan the Devil? Not Jehovah God, because He makes no creature in opposition to him and he makes no lie."[10] Where, then, did Satan come from? He was orginally a spirit creature, an angel, a spirit son of God.

> The one now the Devil was not always such. Time was when he enjoyed a high position in God's family. He was a spirit son of God. Contrary to the opinion of some, he was not an ugly creature with horns and tail, but was beautiful. The Bible figuratively describes him in Ezekiel 28:12, 13: "Thou sealest up the sum, full of wisdom, and perfect in beauty. Thou hast been in Eden the garden of God; every precious stone was thy covering."[11]

This view is similar to that of many born-again Christians. However, the above quote then goes on to state that in keeping with this high angel's position as a son of God, he was given a position of responsibility and trust, "that of overseer of humankind."[12] This belief that Satan was the overseer of humankind is a Witness distinctive.

The Fall of Satan. For a time all went well throughout the universe. There was perfect peace and righteousness. But it did not last. Satan fell because of greed:

> Greed and avariciousness entered in. The coveting cherub had great visions. He saw a race of human creatures on a perfect earth,

all with one accord giving their every devotion to Jehovah and acknowledging him as the great King and Giver of everything good. He wanted that devotion and worship for himself, and so his heart became malicious. He rebelled against the theocratic arrangement. This is indicated by the new name given to him, namely Satan, for that name means "opposer."[13]

Again, many Bible-believing Christians would take a similar view of the fall of Satan. However, Satan's rebellion against the "theocratic arrangement" certainly has a Watchtower flavor.

By this rebellion, he "made a Devil out of himself."[14] He is thus "a self-made Devil."[15] He then used the serpent in Eden to mislead Eve.

The Nature of Satan. At the time of his rebellion against God, Satan's heart became malicious. He is self-admiring and self-seeking. He is cunning and stealthful. He is a liar and "entirely incapable of being a universal ruler like the Most High God."[16] He is a false accuser, misrepresenter and slanderer of God. He is a wicked rebel.

The Work of Satan. Since his fall, it has been Satan's program to overthrow Jehovah's universal sovereignty. He does this by enticing men away from Jehovah. However, he has never been entirely successful. The demons who follow him form an organization. The most aggressive and capable among them have been given superior positions as demon princes who are over the political powers of the earth.[17] The remainder serve under these chief demons. Thus, there is a demon hierarchy under Satan.

Satan's work has been to turn men from God and to prove that he can do so with every human being:

> He turned the first pair away from God in disgrace, and he now reasoned that he was able to turn all human offspring into rebellion against Jehovah's universal sovereignty. He now appeared to have grounds for tauntingly addressing God and challenging him with the words: "Jehovah, you are not able to put on earth men whom I can not by some means turn away from you."[18]

If we should ask, "Where in Scripture do you find any ground that Satan said this?" the answer comes back from the Watchtower, "Those words do not actually appear in the Bible, but the evidence that he said them in effect is clear and unmistakable."[19]

The Doom of Satan. The doom of Satan was first prophesied in Genesis 3:15, which states that the seed of the woman would bruise the serpent's head. The woman in this chapter and verse is Eve. The Watchtower, however, has come up with a new "woman." "The woman was not disobedient Eve, but rather God's heavenly organization of faithful spirit creatures."[20] The woman turns out to be a group of angels. This organization of angels has produced seed, and the chief seed is Christ, Who bruised Satan's head at the time of the cross. This idea fits Witness theology, which says that Christ was orginally an angel. But we find that there is another seed as well. We are told that the Jehovah's Witnesses are also the seed of

God's "woman" and are persecuted by Satan. This teaching that the seed is both Christ and the Jehovah's Witnesses certainly did not come from the Bible!

Satan's doom was not executed back in Eden because "the cherub rebel must have time to bring forth some seed."[21] Satan's doom was partially executed from 1914 to 1918. At that time Michael (who to the Witnesses is Christ in His present form) had a war with Satan, and Satan was cast down from Heaven to earth. This deposing of Satan is a reference to the vision of John in Revelation 12:7–9 in which Satan is referred to as the dragon. It is still future. But for the Witnesses, "the evidence is plentiful that this vision was realized during A.D. 1914–1918."[22]

At this point there is a little confusion in Watchtower literature. On the one hand Satan was "ousted from heaven at [the] Kingdom's establishment,"[23] that is, during the years 1914–1918. Yet on the other hand the Witnesses say the millennial Kingdom is still future in our day.

During the Millennium, Satan will be confined. "Revelation 20:1–3 tells us of the time when the archdeceiver will be completely restrained from his activity. He will be bound and abyssed for a thousand years. . . ."[24] After the thousand years he is loosed, leads a rebellion and is destroyed in the Lake of Fire. Notice, he is not *confined* to the Lake of Fire for eternity, according to the Watchtower; he is utterly destroyed. "Satan will be dead!"[25] And he will not merely be dead; he simply will not exist, period. "The ultimate end of Satan is complete annihilation."[26]

Demonology

Satan is not the only wicked spirit being who is opposed to God. He has demons to help him. What does the Watchtower say about their origin and doom?

The Origin of Demons. The origin of demons was similar to that of Satan in that they were spirit creatures. They came from among the sons of God in the heavens. The Witnesses hold that demons are Satan's seed, and that the time when the demons fell was the period just before Noah's flood. Whalen, commenting on the Witness view, writes:

> Disobedient angels had sexual intercourse with human females and gave birth to freaks and giants known as Nephilim. Finally in disgust Jehovah decided to wipe out all mankind except for the upright Noah and his family. The Witnesses pinpoint the date of the flood in the year 2370 B.C.[27]

Here is the account in the Watchtower's own words:

> The Bible record of Genesis 6:1–5 explains that before the flood of Noah's day some of these spirit "sons of God" materialized as men, that is, they left their place in heaven as spirit creatures and clothed themselves with fleshly bodies. And why? To enjoy human passions by marrying the good-looking daughters of men. . . . By their rebellious action, those spirit sons of God turned themselves into demons and put themselves on the side of the Devil, who is the "ruler of the demons"—Matthew 9:34.[28]

The Witnesses hold that at the time of the flood the demons dissolved their fleshly bodies and returned to the spirit realm, but they were not allowed to rejoin God's organization.

The Doom of Demons. Once back in Heaven, the demons were degraded to a very low state called Tartarus. According to the Watchtower, their imprisonment in Tartarus does not mean confinement in a *place*. Instead they are imprisoned in that they "cannot materialize anymore and live like husbands with women."[29] However, "they still keep as close as they can to mankind, especially to women, whom they prevail upon to serve as spirit mediums, fortune-tellers, clairvoyants, and so forth."[30] With the help of these demons Satan is misleading the earth.

Their ultimate doom is that they will be destroyed along with Satan. Again, for the Witnesses, this does not mean that the demons will spend eternity in the Lake of Fire but that they will be utterly annihilated.

At this point the Witnesses do not even believe their own New World Translation when it plainly states that the devil and his party will be tormented in the Lake of Fire "for ever and ever." Read the New World version of Revelation 20:10:

> And the Devil who was misleading them was hurled into the lake of fire and sulphur, where both the wild beast and the false prophet already were; and they will be tormented day and night for ever and ever.

> What more can we say?

"Then the LORD God formed man
of dust from the ground, and
breathed into his nostrils the
breath of life; and man became a
living being."
Genesis 2:7, the New American
Standard Version

"O LORD, what is man, that Thou
dost take knowledge of him? Or
the son of man, that Thou dost
think of him?"
Psalm 144:3, the New American
Standard Version

10

ADAM AND HIS DUSTY PAST

ABOUT 2,000 B.C., Job from his ash heap asked the question, "What is man?" (Job 7:17). About a thousand years later, King David, perhaps while sitting on his throne, asked the same question, "What is man?" (Ps. 144:3). Today we are living four millennia after Job, and yet this is still a relevant question. What is man? A great variety of theories have been postulated to answer that question. The evolutionist says man is a glorified animal. What does the Watchtower say? What does the Bible say?

In anthropology, as in other areas of systematic theology, the Witnesses are unorthodox. This is because of their views on the nature of man and the immortality of the soul. But first, let us examine their views on the origin of man.

The Origin of Man

Like fundamentalist Christians, the Jehovah's Witnesses strongly oppose the theory of evolution. One of their books, *Did Man Get Here by Evolution or by Creation?*[1], was written for the purpose of refuting evolution. According to the Witnesses, the earth itself was created billions of years ago, but the six days of Genesis 1 and 2 were not nearly so long ago. Some fundamentalists also hold such a view. At this point the analogy ends, for the Witnesses do not believe the days of Genesis 1 and 2 were literal twenty-four hour days. Rather, each day was seven thousand years long, making the first six days 42,000 years in all. Adam and Eve were created at the end of the sixth day (4026 B.C.), the Witnesses say, and therefore man had existed six thousand years as of the autumn of 1975, at which time Armageddon was to have taken place and the millennial Kingdom was to have begun. These six thousand years plus the millennial Kingdom make up the seven thousand of the seventh day.[2]

Apart from the length of the days, the Witnesses take the Genesis 1 and 2 account quite literally. Another problem, however, as we saw earlier, is their view that man was created by Jehovah and by the angel Michael (who later became Christ) in a working partnership.

The Nature of Man

Fundamental, Biblical theology teaches that man is made up of a material part called the body and an immaterial part called the soul and spirit (by trichotomists) or the soul-spirit (by dichotomists). The Witnesses could in a sense be called "monochotomists," for while orthodoxy teaches that man *has* a body and a soul, the Witnesses teach that man *is* a soul. Hoekema reports their view in these words:

> There can be no soul that exists apart from the body. A man, it is said, *is* a soul; he does not *possess* a soul . . . Jehovah's Witnesses therefore oppose the view that man consists of a body and soul; they teach that man is a soul which consists of a body together with a life principle which actuates it.[3]

It may seem strange, but Witness theology asserts that the soul includes the body too. "A human is a soul; he does not possess a soul separate and distinct from the body."[4] Or again, "The soul, then, is indeed the entire person, every fiber of his being, along with his characteristics—his entire personality."[5]

For support the Witnesses like to turn to Genesis 2:7, "And the LORD God formed man of the dust of the ground, and breathed into his nostrils the breath of life; and *man became a living soul*" [italics mine]. There, that proves it, doesn't it? No. The problem springs from the Hebrew word *nephesh*. This word sometimes means *soul*, but often it means *person, being, creature, self, life*, etc. It must always be interpreted in the context of the chapter and verse in which it is found. The Witnesses fail to distinguish between the verses where *nephesh* refers to soul in an absolute sense (and thus should be translated *soul*) and the verses where this word refers to a person, self, life, etc. Thus they make statements such as "the Bible says that the soul 'needs to eat',"[6] when actually it is a person who needs to eat.

In Genesis 2:7, the King James Version translates the last phrase "and man became a living soul," but it should be translated "and man became a living being." This is how both the New American Standard Bible and the New International Version render the phrase, and it makes the meaning clear. First, God formed man's body of the dust of the ground, but at that point there was no life in it. Then God breathed the breath of life into this body and man became alive. He was now a living being.

It is this same failure to distinguish between the various meanings of *nephesh* that led the Watchtower to write, "the claim of religionists that man has an immortal soul, and therefore differs from the beast is not Scriptural. The Bible shows that both man and beast are souls."[7] Not so! The Bible uses the word *nephesh* for animals on occasion, but in the context of animals it means *creature* or *life*, not *soul*. The New World Translation is in error in its translation of Genesis 1:24 when it says:

> Let the earth put forth living *souls* according to their kinds, domestic animals and moving animals and wild beast of the earth according to its kind [italics mine].[8]

Nephesh here should be translated *creature*:
"Let the earth bring forth the living creature after his kind" (AV).
"Let the land produce living creatures according to their kinds" (NIV).
"Let the earth bring forth living creatures after their kind" (NASV).
Members of the mineral kingdom do not have

life at all. Above the mineral kingdom is the vegetable kingdom. Its members have life, but not animated life. Above the vegetable kingdom is the animal kingdom. Its members not only have life, but animated life—they can move about. Above the animal kingdom is the highest creature with a physical body—man. Not only does he have life and animated life, he also has a soul and spirit and was made in the image of God (Gen. 1:27).

The Watchtower, denying this truth, asserts, "the fact is that the entire Bible teaches that man *is* a soul" [italics in original].[9] But if the soul includes the entire man, why did Paul state, "I pray God your whole spirit and soul and body be preserved blameless unto the coming of our Lord Jesus Christ" (1 Thess. 5:23)? Why did he not simply pray that the soul would be preserved? The Witnesses' reply that Paul is referring to (1) the spirit of the Thessalonian congregation, and (2) the soul of that congregation and (3) the body of that congregation is simply another attempt to force Watchtower beliefs on the Bible. It is reading into the passage something that is not there. The Thessalonian "congregation" was not preserved until the second coming of Christ.

The truth of the matter is that the Bible shows that man has a soul that is distinct from the body and dwells within a person.

Positive proof of this can be seen in Job 14:22—"his flesh upon him shall have pain, and his soul within him shall mourn." Other scriptures verifying this same truth read as follows: "And the man of God said, let her alone; for her soul is vexed within her" (2 Kings 4:27). The Psalmist cries out: "Why art thou cast down, O my soul? and why art thou disquieted in me?" (Psalm 42:5). These scriptures prove beyond any shadow of doubt that man certainly has a soul within him.[10]

The Immortality of Man's Soul

Not only does the Watchtower Society differ with the Bible on the ingredients of the nature of man, it also differs on the destiny of those ingredients. Orthodoxy teaches that man's soul will continue to exist forever. This belief is sometimes called "the immortality of the soul," though technically speaking immortality refers to man's body (cf. 1 Cor. 15:50–54). However:

> What Scripture does support is that man once created does possess a quality (soul or spirit) which can exist as a conscious entity apart from the body and which will continue in its existence through all eternity.[11]

The doctrine of the inherent immortality of the soul is bitterly opposed by the Witnesses. They say that scientists and surgeons cannot find evidence that man has an immortal soul. This is the same type of argument Russian communist astronauts used to try to prove there was no God!

The Witnesses say that this teaching, like that of the Trinity, is of the devil: "Thus it is seen that the serpent [the Devil] is the one that originated the doctrine of the inherent immortality of human souls."[12] They believe that this is the foundational doctrine of false religion.

The Witnesses teach that when a person dies, he ceases to exist in an absolute sense. "Death means total annihilation and there are no souls waiting anywhere for a resurrection, but after the parousia all the dead will be *recreated* and brought back to earth."[13] This Watchtower doctrine, of course, fits in nicely with its views of hell and the ultimate destiny of the wicked. If man simply ceases to exist in any form at death, and if his soul and spirit as well as his body become entirely nonexistent, then there can be no conscious suffering in the next world.

To the Witnesses, immortality belongs only to the faithful: "Immortality is a reward for faithfulness. It does not come automatically to a human at birth."[14] It is said that even Jesus did not have an immortal soul but was granted immortality because of His obedience and faithfulness to God the Father.

The Bible, however, indicates that at death the believer is not annihilated to be later recreated. Rather, the departed believer goes to be with the Lord. Paul states, "We are confident, I say, and willing rather to be absent from the body, and to be present with the Lord" (2 Cor. 5:8).

At this point, a word should be added about the immaterial part of man called the spirit. To the Witnesses, this is simply a life principle which activates the body to form a complete soul or being.

The Image of God in Man

The Witnesses declare that man was created in the image of God, which means that he is a higher form of creature than the animals. Originally he was given dominion over the animals, and he had God's attributes.

According to the express statement of the Creator himself, man was made in the image of God. Not that man had the same form and substance as his Creator, but that he had God's attributes. To man as a creature with God's attributes was granted the privilege of holding dominion over the earth and its form of life: the birds, fish and animals.[15]

A more orthodox view would point out that the image of God includes the personal image: that both God and man possess personality; that the image of God includes endless being; that it includes intellect; that it includes a moral nature. Orthodoxy would also point out that the image of God in man was marred by the Fall.

The Fall of Man

The Witnesses do not simply teach that Adam was created innocent; they teach that he was created perfect. Most orthodox theologians teach that if Adam had not sinned he would have been confirmed in righteousness and thus would have become positively holy and would have lived forever. According to the Witnesses' view, if Adam had not sinned he could have lived forever though mortal.[16] Thus he would never have gained immortality and yet would have lived on the earth forever. As such, he would have been forever dependent upon food. However, Adam disobeyed Jehovah.

The Witnesses accept the account of the Fall given in Genesis 3 as a literal event, but they teach that when Satan saw Adam and Eve worshipping God he became covetous and thus fell. He then tempted Eve and she in turn got Adam to fall.

As a result of the Fall, Adam and Eve lost their perfection. Their descendants, thus, are born imperfect. "Thus Adam lost for himself, and for the human souls that would come after him, perfection, eternal life and the paradise of Eden."[17] It is the goal of today's Jehovah's Witness to reach a paradise that covers the whole earth.[18] If Adam and Eve had not sinned, they and their descendants would have eventually been able to push the boundaries of Eden to the ends of the earth, according to the Witnesses. However, Adam lost it all.

Another result of Adam's fall was death. Death meant absolute annihilation for him, not a separation of soul and body. "There is nothing to indicate that God meant that sinner Adam would only appear to die but that his soul would live on forever."[19] When Adam died, he went nowhere but back to the dust from which he had been taken, according to the Watchtower. He will not be resurrected because he was a willful sinner. He has simply ceased to be, as if he never was.

"The heart is deceitful above all
————— things, and desperately wicked: —————
who can know it?"
Jeremiah 17:9

11

THE DECEITFUL HEART

SIN is a very small word, but it has had a tremendous effect on man ever since Adam partook of the forbidden fruit. The doctrine of sin is called hamartiology by theologians. What is sin? It can be defined as anything contrary to the character of God. Christian Science says sin is an illusion, for according to Mary Baker Eddy, "Man is incapable of sin, sickness, and death."[1] The Bible nonetheless plainly asserts that man is a sinner, "For all have sinned, and come short of the glory of God" (Rom. 3:23). What do the Witnesses teach about sin?

The Nature of Sin

The Witnesses teach that sin is a falling short of God's mark of perfection. It is a transgression of the law of God. Such falling short may be due to fleshly imperfection, a wayward tendency, with

which all are born. Sin may also be due to igno-
rance. Sin results in death, which for the Witnesses means annihilation. However, most who are
annihilated will be re-created. Those who will not
be re-created are Adam, Cain, Judas Iscariot and
Jehovah's Witnesses who left the fold, as well as
some who sinned willfully.

The Witnesses do not write as much about sin
as they do the other topics of theology. They do
believe that all are sinners, but they do not often
point out sin in the life of the individual. Usually the Watchtower speaks about the sinful conditions of the world, contrasting them with the
eventual paradisiacal earth conditions. For example, "World conditions never looked blacker."[2]
"Many youngsters appear to be robbing and rap-
ing, maiming and murdering as casually as they
go to a movie or join a pickup baseball game."[3]

Original Sin

The Witnesses believe in original sin. By Adam's disobedience he brought death not only on
himself but upon the whole human race. Adam
and Eve sinned by disobeying a plainly stated law
of God. "No descendant of Adam is free from sin;
all inherit it from [the] first man."[4] This sin of
Adam causes his descendants to be born with an
inherited disability and an inherited condemnation.[5]

The Cure for Sin

The Witnesses believe that the cure for sin is
made possible through the death of Christ. Those
who commit sin should make confession and seek
forgiveness from God through Christ. Any course
that leads to sin should be avoided. All of this

sounds quite Biblical until it comes to the matter of the ransom paid for sin. The Watchtower teaches that Jesus Christ forfeited His perfect human (not divine) life as a ransom for men who believe. This ransom offsets their inherited condemnation when it is applied to their merit. We will save our comments on this for the next chapter.

"But she *wanted* to die. I was convinced that she wanted to die mainly because she couldn't do the witness work and she wanted to *endure faithfully to the end*" [italics in original].
Joe Hewitt,
"Mama Got Her Wish,"
I Was Raised a Jehovah's Witness,
p. 87

12

SALVATION IS NOT FOREVER

ONE of the favorite verses of the Watchtower seems to be Matthew 24:13, "But he that shall endure unto the end, the same shall be saved." A major principle of sound, Biblical interpretation is that a verse of Scripture should *always* be interpreted in its context. The context of this verse is Christ's Olivet Discourse (see Matt. 24:3) which covers chapters 24 and 25. This great discourse deals with end-time events (again see Matt. 24:3). It must be remembered, therefore, that Christ is not telling us how to be saved in this message but rather what the endtime will be like. In the first part of this discourse, the Lord is describing the tribulation period (notice vv. 21 and 29). It is in this setting that Matthew 24:13 is placed. What Christ is teaching is that the tribulation period will be one of severe persecution. Some who have been saved in that period will die (Matt. 24:9, "Then shall they deliver you up to be afflicted, and shall kill you . . ."). Not all will be killed, however, and the ones surviving to the end will be *delivered* (as the word *hupomeinas* could better be translated) from destruction and death and will go on into the Kingdom. Christ was speaking of *physical* salvation, *physical* deliverance during the tribulation period. He was not speaking of spiritual salvation during the Church Age.

However, the Watchtower has latched onto Matthew 24:13 as a whip to keep the troops working, working, working. With that view of the verse as a backdrop, we do well to ask, What else does the Watchtower teach about soteriology, the doctrine of salvation?

Although the Witnesses make much propaganda out of not having a clergy class (even this is changing, however) and a laity class, they do have two classes of people. This caste system is far more rigid. The two classes are the 144,000 or Little Flock, and the Great Crowd or the rest of the Witnesses. Nowhere does this caste system come to light more than in the doctrines of salvation and the church. In soteriology it is so major that it is necessary to develop the discussion around these two groups of Jehovah's Witnesses. This we will do following a quick look at their beliefs about the need for salvation and the provision for it.

The Need for Salvation

The Fall brought death to all men. Adam and Eve lost the possibility of perfect human life with all its rights and earthly prospects. "Earthly prospects" has a Witness flavor. Man now has an inherited disability and an inherited condemnation. All men are in need of salvation.[1]

The Provision for Salvation

Jehovah is the Provider of salvation, according to Witness theology, and Jesus Christ is the Chief Agent through Whom salvation comes. On the "torture stake" (the cross without a cross bar) Jesus made an atonement for sin. He did this by providing the ransom price. It was "a perfect human life sacrificed for a perfect human life lost."[2] Actually, in the Watchtower system it was *one* perfect human life sacrificed for *millions* of imperfect humans. So it was not really a "corresponding ransom," which is what the Witnesses would have us believe.

The Witnesses would also have us believe that Christ was nothing more than a perfect man. They say that if He had been both God and a perfect man He could not have been an acceptable ransom, for that would have been more than God's justice demanded. They seem to forget the infinite holiness of God and the enormity of sin.

For the Witnesses, Christ, as a perfect man, made this sacrifice. It was a sacrifice because He did it willingly.[3] He did not have to die; He willingly forfeited His perfect human life and thus gave men the opportunity to live. Therefore, Christ could not have taken up His human life at the time of His resurrection, for that would have nullified the ransom.

Limited versus Unlimited Atonement

The Witnesses teach a modified form of unlimited atonement. They say that Christ made it possible for most of mankind to secure salvation.

However, there is no hope for certain individuals and certain groups. First, there is no hope for Adam, who particularly comes under fire in Witness literature:

> The man Adam is not included in those ransomed. Why not? Because he was a willful sinner, was justly sentenced to death, and died deservedly, and God would not reverse his just judgment and give Adam life. He had a perfect life, and this he deliberately forfeited. There is no provision in God's ransom for Adam.[4]

Neither is there any hope for Cain, the people of Noah's day or Judas Iscariot. Thrown into this class also are Jehovah's Witnesses who have left the fold. This teaching is another scare tactic to keep the "brothers and sisters" in line.

Universalism

The Witnesses take a stand against universal salvation. They rightly describe it as unscriptural. It is plainly stated that not everyone will gain final salvation.[5] On the other hand, it should be remembered that they also teach that no one will be eternally lost in the sense of suffering everlasting punishment. Those who are not saved at death simply cease to be.

Salvation of the 144,000

At this point we must divide the topic of salvation into two parts, for the Watchtower teaches a vastly different way of salvation for the Little Flock (the 144,000) than it does for the rest of the Jehovah's Witnesses, the Great Crowd. Those of the 144,000, also called the Spiritual Temple class, must believe and repent. To repent is to have a change of mind regarding sin and this wicked world.[6] Faith is defined by the Watchtower in *Let God Be True* on pages 295–96 (revised edition):

> Faith means that by reason of Bible knowledge one has a firm assurance that God exists and that he will reward those who earnestly seek him, and that the Bible is his truth and man's sure guide. It further means to accept Jesus not only as a Teacher and Example but also as one's Savior and Ransomer. Such faith causes one to be converted or turned, to change his course of action.[7]

Accepting Jesus as one's Savior and Ransomer does not sound too far from orthodoxy until it is remembered that to the Witnesses, Christ as the Ransomer was not God but only a perfect man.

This faith is demonstrated by total dedication—unconditional surrender—to Jehovah. It is to be followed by baptism by immersion. The Witnesses go on to teach that following dedication, Christ covers the sins of the one dedicating himself, so that he can then be justified by God and have access to God through Christ. God then causes the individual to be anointed with His active force (the Holy Spirit) and he becomes God's spiritual son.

Thus, according to the Watchtower, these of the anointed class are "born again." The Society teaches that only the 144,000 persons are to seek and receive the "born-again" experience, and the rest are actually to remain unregenerate, for theirs is an earthly hope.[8]

This select group of 144,000 makes up the Congregation of God. They are also "the body of Christ" and "the bride of the Lamb." They are the spiritual Israelites, and they will be rewarded by means of a resurrection to spirit life. They have a hope of life in Heaven. It is a hope of *Heaven* because, unlike the Great Crowd, they believe they are Heaven bound.

It is only a *hope* of Heaven, however, because they must carry out their dedication to Jehovah—that is, do good works here on earth—faithfully until death to actually get there. If they should turn back from this dedication, such a turning back "would mark them as agreement-breakers, worthy of death, annihilation."[9] (Remember, they must "endure to the end" to be saved!)

The 144,000 do not go to Heaven, however, because of Christ's sacrifice. That was only the first step. They get there because of their own sacrifice:

> Another point should here be noted. What Christ earned by his ransom, as we have seen, was a perfect human life with its rights and earthly prospects. When the anointed ones are justified, they receive this right to perfect life on earth. This right, however, they now proceed to sacrifice by giving up their bodies fit for life on earth and their right to perfect life on earth, as Jesus had done before them; by so doing they obtain the right to share heavenly life, with Christ after death. Thus they obtain the right to heavenly life, not through Christ's sacrifice since He earned

only the right to perfect life on earth, but through their own sacrifice of their earthly prospects in the Paradise of the New World. It is therefore literally true that these 144,000 *earn their own way* to Heaven [italics mine].[10]

Salvation of the Great Crowd

The Other Sheep or the Great Crowd are the Witnesses who joined the movement after the 144,000 was complete, which took place somewhere around the year 1931.[11] These Witnesses too must have faith in Jehovah and in Jesus Christ. They too must dedicate themselves to do the will of God and must faithfully carry out their dedication. Furthermore, they too must be baptized by immersion, which symbolizes complete dedication.

The Watchtower states that these Witnesses cannot be born again. They are not saved, neither are they seeking to be saved. Their hope is to live on earth eternally. They will not be justified until the Millennium is over. God does not regenerate them, consecrate them or sanctify them.[12] "They do not expect to go to Heaven. They have been promised everlasting life on earth, including the privilege of subduing, beautifying and populating the earth, if they, as Jehovah's Witnesses, prove their faithfulness [remember, endure to the end!] to him before his war of Armageddon."[13]

This, then, is the "salvation" today's Jehovah's Witnesses are offered! Instead of the prospect of an eternity in the presence of our great God and Savior Jesus Christ in the glories of Heaven, they hope to spend eternity subduing the earth! Never have so many worked so hard for so little.

Furthermore, they are taught that if they do not keep working, they will lose even this hope.

Eternal Insecurity

The Watchtower does not believe in the perseverance of the saints, or "once saved, always saved." The Witnesses might get lazy that way. Rather, endurance is required.[14] The Witnesses are taught that they must prove themselves worthy: "Their faithfulness must be shown by performing their commission to preach in spite of any and all opposition, and in this way they prove their trustworthiness as Jesus did."[15] The Jehovah's Witnesses' religion is a religion of works, which to some degree accounts for the zeal of the Watchtower advocates. They must endure to the end.

The Witnesses follow the pattern started by Cain of old. This son of Adam tried to approach God with the fruit of his own efforts, which was rejected by God (Gen. 4:3, 5). Abel instead came to God by way of the blood of a lamb, and he was accepted by God (Gen. 4:4).

Instead of coming to God by way of the shed blood of the Lamb, Jesus Christ, the Witnesses seek to come by faith *plus* works. For them, finally obtaining eternal life depends on dedication and human effort: "All who by reason of faith in Jehovah God and in Christ Jesus dedicate themselves to do God's will *and then faithfully carry out their dedication* will be rewarded with everlasting life" [italics mine].[16]

The Watchtower system is eternal insecurity and a salvation that may not last forever. The Biblical system is salvation by grace apart from hu-

man effort since Christ has already paid the full
price:

> For by *grace* are ye saved through *faith*; and
> that *not of yourselves*: it is the gift of God:
> *Not of works*, lest any man should boast (Eph.
> 2:8, 9).

> Forasmuch as ye know that ye were not re-
> deemed with corruptible things, as silver and
> gold, from your vain conversation received
> by tradition from your fathers;
> But with the *precious blood of Christ*, as of
> a lamb without blemish and without spot (1
> Pet. 1:18, 19).

> This kind of salvation is forever!

> And I give unto them eternal life; and they
> shall *never* perish, neither shall any man
> pluck them out of my hand (John 10:28).

> Now unto *him* that is *able to keep you from
> falling*, and to present you faultless before
> the presence of his glory with exceeding joy
> (Jude 24).

"Since the national congregation of Israel was, when faithful, a prophetic type of the Christian 'congregation of God,' the rule of God's congregation of spiritual Israel must likewise be theocratic, not democratic, not congregational." Watchtower Bible and Tract Society, *Life Everlasting in Freedom of the Sons of God*, pp. 168, 169

13

THE CONGREGATION
OF GOD

ECCLESIOLOGY may be defined as a study of the Scriptures concerning the church. Orthodox theologians speak in terms of two categories in dealing with this subject: (1) the Church universal and (2) the local church. The Church universal is the complete Body of Christ existing in every place. The local church is an individual assembly meeting in one locality.

Let us examine what the Witnesses believe about these two categories.

The Church Universal

In studying the cults, one soon finds that they do not believe in such a thing as a Church universal. Most, if not all of them, believe that they are the *only true* religious organization. Listen to the Mormons:

From the facts already stated, it is evident that the Church was literally driven from the earth; in the first ten centuries immediately following the ministry of Christ, the authority of the priesthood was lost from among men, and no human power could restore it. But the Lord in His mercy provided for the re-establishment of His Church in the last days, and for the last time. . . . It has been already shown that this restoration was effected by the Lord through the Prophet Joseph Smith.[1]

How about this concerning The Way, International:

Dr. Wierwille's "special discoveries" placed us a notch above other Christians. Revealed to him through his Bible study, they had to be true. And didn't God speak audibly to him? "The greatest man of God since the Apostle Paul" [by his evaluation] taught us several doctrinal teachings which were used to establish continuity and unity.[2]

Or this from Herbert W. Armstrong, founder of the Worldwide Church of God:

It is, I know, a shocking, staggering FACT to realize that this work—*The* PLAIN TRUTH, *The World Tomorrow* program on radio world-wide and on daily TV in the U.S. (and Canada weekly)—the work going on from Ambassador College and the Worldwide Church of God, is the ONLY WORK ON EARTH proclaiming the very gospel of Jesus Christ to the world in great power![3]

It is not unusual for a cult to loudly proclaim, "We alone have the truth. We alone are the true church." This is also the Witnesses' attitude. The Watchtower states that it is the only *true* religious organization. "This means that Christ is using only one organization on earth to bring spiritual food to the people."[4]

All other religious bodies are fiercely attacked by the Witnesses. The clergy of other groups are sneeringly called *religionists*. And in Rutherford's words, "All liars and murderers are religionists."[5] Again he wrote, "The clergy do not in fact represent God and Christ but do represent God's enemy, the Devil."[6] Nor has this attitude died with Rutherford. A *Watchtower* article of 1975 declares, "While Christendom's clergy have sought to elevate themselves to a godlike position, many things that they themselves have done are most ungodly."[7]

Because the Watchtower organization is the "one and only true congregation of God," there is no interchurch fellowship or cooperation of any kind. Yet, Witness books are advertised as "nonsectarian" literature.

The Witnesses interpret 1 Corinthians 1:10, in which Paul tells the Corinthian local church not to be divided, to mean that the whole church worldwide can have no divisions. "So we cannot Scripturally expect to find them [members of the true church] scattered among all the conflicting religions of Christendom. They must be gathered together in just one organization."[8] That one organization, of course, is none other than the Watchtower organization.

God's Word teaches that the real congregation of God is made up of those who have been regenerated by the Holy Spirit because they have received Jesus Christ as their own personal Savior. "But as many as received him, to them gave he power to become the sons of God, even to them that believe on his name" (John 1:12). That is straight from the Bible.

The "true" church of the Witnesses, however, does not include all Christians. In fact, it apparently does not even include all the Jehovah's Witnesses:

> This is the "church of the firstborn who are *written in the heavens.*" God is the one who selects the members. . . . And Jesus revealed that, far from including all who profess to be Christians, they are limited in number to 144,000.—Revelation 14:1–3; Luke 12:32 [italics in original].[9]

The true church was founded at Pentecost in the year 33 C.E. (the common era—the Witnesses no longer use A.D.). Jesus Christ is the foundation of it. However, say the Witnesses, the church has become "Abraham's Seed"[10] and, as spiritual Israel, all the Old Testament promises to natural Israel are transferred to the Watchtower organization. Any relationship between God and natural Israel has been nullified.

The other Jehovah's Witnesses, although they are not part of the true church, and although they cannot take part in the Lord's Evening Meal, (i.e., communion), serve with the remnant of the 144,000 who are still around. "Even as those of the true church or congregation faithfully walk in Christ's footsteps and proclaim the Kingdom message, so likewise these sheeplike ones 'go with them' serving God right along with them."[11]

The Local Church

The Jehovah's Witnesses call their local assemblies congregations. In Rutherford's day they were called companies. In the past the Witnesses usually met in homes or in rented halls. Now more local congregations are erecting their own buildings, called Kingdom Halls. These usually are modest structures. They are simply meeting places for the Witnesses and are not considered to be the house of God. The Witnesses would rather put their money into literature.

In Russell's day, the local churches were independent units. Much of Rutherford's efforts were directed toward bringing them under the thumb of the Watchtower headquarters. Although he drove many out, he was successful with those who remained, and today the Watchtower has a rigid hierarchical system. The leaders of the local congregations are no longer elected but instead are appointed by headquarters. Only those who never deviate from official policy or doctrine can expect to get ahead.

A Witness who falls out of favor with the organization for some reason may be "disfellowshipped." "A disfellowshipped person is cut off from the congregation, and the congregation has nothing to do with him. Those in the congregation will not extend the hand of fellowship to this one, nor will they so much as say 'Hello' or 'Good-bye' to him. He is not welcome in their private homes."[12]

This discipline period lasts for a year. If the offender submits in humility, he will then need to meet with a committee which hears the matter. "If he satisfies them of his change of heart, they will probably decide to reinstate him in the congregation. But he will never be used in any position of responsibility in the congregation again, as he can never be considered completely trust-worthy."[13] This does not say much for the Watchtower's attitude toward forgiveness. It is a good thing for the apostle Peter that he was not a Jehovah's Witness! (See Mark 14:66–72 and Acts 2:14 ff.)

Until recently the Witnesses had no ordained clergy. All active Witnesses were called ministers. The presiding minister or leader of the local congregation was called the congregational servant or overseer.

Not only does church policy come down from the top, but so does Bible interpretation. The Witness headquarters at Brooklyn has the complete and final say as to what every verse in the Bible means. The Witness is expected to accept everything the Watchtower puts out as gospel truth. "He dare not find one error in any current Watchtower material! Nor dare he successfully contradict anything the Watchtower ever says."[14]

At times some Witnesses do study the Bible for themselves and not simply through Watchtower literature. Often, when they see how the Society misinterprets and twists Scripture, they leave the organization. (The number is now reported to be in the thousands.[15] For additional information see footnote 16 of this chapter.) The Society may retaliate by disfellowshipping the "wrongdoer"—one final threat to keep the troops in line.

The Two Ordinances

The Witnesses baptize by immersion. This may be done in a mass ceremony, which is good for publicity. Baptism, surprisingly, is in the name

of the Father and of the Son and of the holy spirit
(again, not Holy Spirit).

This means they must recognize Jehovah not
only as their life-giver but also as the Supreme One to whom they owe allegiance and
service. They must recognize the part the
Son performs in Jehovah's purpose and what
he has done for them. They must also recognize the holy spirit as the active force of God
which will help them to carry out their dedication and that they are at all times to act
in harmony with it.[17]

It can be seen from the above that the Witnesses' baptism, while it is in the name of the Persons of the Trinity (which they deny), still does not
constitute valid baptism, for it does not picture
the participant's union with Christ in His death,
burial and resurrection (see Col. 2:12).

Communion, or the Lord's Evening Meal, is
observed by the remnant of the "true church," the
Witnesses who make up the 144,000. At this point
in Witness history they are elderly people, and
there are very few of them left on earth. The Witness who comes knocking on your door undoubtedly is not allowed to take part in this service
because he/she is part of the Great Crowd instead.

Communion is considered a memorial, which
is Scriptural (1 Cor. 11:25, 26). However, the
Watchtower argues that it can only be held once
a year, on the 14th of Nisan. They claim that as
a memorial it *must be* on the anniversary of the
first Lord's Supper. Again, both reason and the
Bible prove them wrong. An event may be remembered more than once a year; it is illogical

to argue otherwise. Most of all, the Bible proves them to be wrong. Acts 20:7 shows that the early disciples broke bread on the *first day of the week*, even though the anniversary of the Lord's Supper would not always come on the first day of the week. Moreover, the tense of the Greek verb translated "came together" indicates it was something they habitually did on the first day of the week. The early church did not practice the Lord's Supper only once a year! We should always go to the *Bible* as our source of authority.

"In JW material I discovered many false prophecies. Our leaders had received messages from God that the world would end in 1874, 1879, 1881, 1914, 1925 and 1941. (Even in 1980 one issue of the *Watchtower* apologized for disappointing so many people by announcing 1975 as the end-of-the-world date.)"

William Cetnar,
Escape from Darkness, p. 35

14

AT THE SOUND OF
THE TRUMPET

"THE Witnesses make the Millennium the center of everything religious."[1] Its eschatology has been the major point of propaganda throughout its history. Russell's first book published in 1877 already had set a date for Christ's coming. One of Rutherford's earliest books (1920) was called *Millions Now Living Will Never Die!* and concerned the end time. A 1975 issue of *Awake!* has a cover caption stating, "An earthly paradise: Why you can hope to see it." The magazine carries three major articles on the same subject.[2]

In dealing with the Witness doctrines of last things, our study will center around five topics: the second advent of Christ, the battle of Armageddon, the Millennium, the final overthrow of Satan and the eternal state. If the reader does not know what the Witnesses teach about the end of the age and the eternity beyond, he may be in for some real surprises!

The Second Advent of Christ

The Witnesses believe in a second advent of Christ. This belief can be misleading, however, for as with so many of their other doctrines, they do not view the Second Advent at all in the orthodox sense of the term. In fact, even their terminology is different.

Terminology Used. The Witnesses usually do not speak of the second *coming* of Christ. They prefer to speak of the second *presence* of Christ. This term fits in better with their view that it occurred over seventy years ago, and that He has been present ever since. Strictly speaking, "His coming or return marks the beginning of his presence."[3]

The Manner of His Advent. To the Witnesses, this coming or presence of Christ was not a visible, physical return at all. "His second presence does not need some visible evidence for us to discern it, because he must be present invisibly as a glorious immortal spirit. The purpose of his second presence requires it to be invisible."[4]

The belief in an invisible, spiritual return of Christ is not new within the movement. It was over this very point that Russell broke with the little Adventist group in 1875 and joined Barbour (see page 21).

The Meaning of His Advent. If Christ's advent was not a visible, physical return to the earth, then what was it? The Witness answer is, "Christ's return being for him to rule in the Kingdom, then his second coming means his entering actively into the power of the Kingdom."[5] After Christ's second advent took place secretly in 1914 (according to the Watchtower), Christ came to His spiritual temple and began cleansing it. This cleansing began to take place in 1918.

The Seventh-day Adventists use the same excuse to justify Miller's unfulfilled prediction of the 1844 return of Christ:

> If Daniel 8:14 showed that Christ must have returned in 1844, well, then He did return in 1844. And if He had not returned to this earth, well then He had returned somewhere else. In other words, the sanctuary mentioned in Daniel 8:14—"then shall the sanctuary be cleansed," was not on earth. Where was it then? In heaven, of course.[6]

For the Witnesses, Christ's *parousia* began in 1914. It was at the same time that the kingdom of heaven was actually established and Satan was cast out of Heaven:

> Since 1914 world-shattering events have followed one another in quick succession. These mark that year as the time when Christ Jesus began to rule in the midst of his enemies. It was a time when the nations became wrathful. The birth that year of the heavenly government pictured by the male child that would rule all nations with an iron rod precipitated a war in heaven, resulting in the ousting of Satan, who has since then brought great woe to the earth and the sea, just as foretold—Revelation 11:17, 18; 12:1–12, NWT.[7]

Thus the kingdom is now actually here. Christ is right now ruling in power in His kingdom toward earth. (The Witnesses do not speak of His kingdom *over* earth or *in* earth but *toward* earth.)

As mentioned in the excerpt above, the second presence of Christ marked the casting out of Satan from Heaven. This casting out was done by Christ, Who is actually the angel Michael, according to the Watchtower.

Christ's second advent also means that those of the 144,000 who had died prior to 1918 were raised to spirit bodies to join the spirit creature Christ. This event is referred to as a partial rapture, or the first resurrection.[8] Since then all those of the anointed class (the Little Flock) are immediately changed at death to spirit life. They do not go into a period of soul sleep, like the rest of the Witnesses.

Finally, the Second Advent means that the end times have begun. If you were to ask how the kingdom of heaven could already have been established seventy-five years ago and yet things continue as if Christ had not taken over the rule, the Witness answer would be that things are not the same at all. Things are much worse now than before He began ruling, because Satan is at work on earth in these end-time days. At the same time, the established kingdom is being proclaimed. (Evidently it has taken Christ seventy-five years to consolidate His power and the task is not over yet!) Phase one of the established kingdom will end with the battle of Armageddon, when Satan's organization will be overthrown. This battle is near at hand.

The Battle of Armageddon

This next great event in Witness eschatology is eagerly awaited by members of the movement. William J. Whalen, who is quite sympathetic toward the Witnesses, called his book *Armageddon Around the Corner*. The Watchtower uses the nearness of the battle as an extremely effective means of instilling a great urgency in its people to work while there is yet time. In fact, the Watchtower is a master in this area. And no wonder: it has been at it now for over a hundred years!

The Time of the Battle. The time of the battle of Armageddon is vitally tied into the whole eschatological system of the Witnesses. Long ago the Witnesses set the date of the Second Advent at 1914. Because of their interpretation of Matthew 24:33 and 34, in which they take the word "generation" to actually mean generation instead of race, they are forced to say that the battle will be soon.

> So likewise ye, when ye shall see all these things, know that it is near, even at the doors. Verily I say unto you, This generation shall not pass, till all these things be fulfilled (Matt. 24:33, 34).

> We know Armageddon is near for another reason. Jesus said that the generation of people living when the "time of the end" began would not pass away before Armageddon breaks out. . . . Many are the people alive since 1914 who will still be living when it is time for Armageddon to begin.[9]

Having set the beginning of this period at 1914, the Witnesses have had considerable problems.

In 1932 Rutherford was telling his followers that the event was about to happen:

In that year he declared that the religious

work of the Witnesses was "coming to a conclusion," that the end was "only a short time away," and that the end was "much less than the length of a generation."[10]

In 1941 Rutherford wrote a book called *Children*.[11] In this book a young couple put off their marriage until after Armageddon, it was viewed as being so near.

In 1943 the book *The Truth Shall Make You Free* set the date at 1972. In 1966 the date was set for the fall of 1975. As the autumn of that year approached, the Witnesses were ready. The October 15, 1975 issue of *Awake!* said, "The fulfillment of that prophecy is now about to take place. All the present-day national sovereignties on earth will shortly have to bow before the Messianic kingdom in the hands of the heavenly Son of God."[12] Nothing happened, of course, and another Witness prediction failed to materialize! The "autumn of 1975" failure has been a bitter pill for the Watchtower to swallow. How did the Watchtower arrive at that date?

The Watchtower teaches that the days of creation of Genesis 1 and 2 are 7,000 years long each. The seventh day, or the day of rest, thus is also to be 7,000 years long. Furthermore, the Witnesses arrived at the year 4026 B.C. as the date of the creation of Adam. The rest was easy. The seventh day includes the millennial Kingdom of 1,000 years duration. Take the 1,000 from the 7,000 and it is 6,000 years from creation to the battle of Armageddon. Six thousand years after 4026 B.C. is A.D. 1975 (a year is lost going from 1 B.C. to 1 A.D.). This time the Witnesses were sure they had the key. But again they were wrong.

A Description of the Battle. Although the Witnesses speak much of the battle of Armageddon, it is not a literal battle to be fought in the land of Palestine:

> Armageddon, then, is not the name of a literal battle field; it is the name of a symbolic one. The literal field of Megiddo in Palestine would be too small to hold all the kings of the earth and their armies. God's war will be fought world-wide. So Armageddon refers to God's war by which he destroys this evil world at the "accomplished end."[13]

The Great Crowd of Jehovah's Witnesses will not be raptured before the battle because they will not be going to Heaven. They will forever remain on earth. Yet at the same time they will not take part in the battle. "Jehovah's Witnesses on earth will not need to take part in Armageddon at all."[14] They will simply be spectators of the event.

On the one side will be Christ at the head of an army of powerful angels. On the other side will be Satan, the demons and Satan's human organization: the United Nations, the leaders of pagan religions and Christendom. The battle will be severe and quick, with an overwhelming victory for Christ and His angels. Those destroyed will be the wicked, religious organizations that misled people and were built on falsehood, political governmental systems and Satan and his demons.[15] Satan and the demons are bound by the angel Christ for a thousand years and hurled into an abyss. "The abyss means a deathlike state of inactivity."[16] This "abyssing" of the devil marks the end of Armageddon. At that time the New World, the millennial reign of Christ, will begin.

The Millennium

The Witnesses teach that the millennial reign of Christ will see Christ ruling over the earth, which will have returned to paradisiacal conditions. Who will make up the Kingdom?

The Inhabitants of the Millennium. There will be a number of different groups who will inhabit the Millennium set up in a paradisiacal earth. Of course, the Jehovah's Witnesses will be there, except for the 144,000, who will be in Heaven reigning with Christ. The Witnesses of the 144,000 who did not die when Armageddon took place will be there during the Millennium until they live out their lives. At that time they will be resurrected to spirit bodies to join the rest of the 144,000 who are in Heaven.

The members of the Great Crowd or Other Sheep, the common Jehovah's Witnesses of today, will survive the holocaust and will enter the Millennium in their natural bodies. The members of the Great Crowd who died prior to Armageddon will be restored to life again. Since they were *annihilated* at death, God will have to *re-create* them, all according to His memory. How these new ones who are re-created, not brought back to life, can be the same ones who died and were annihilated tests our reasoning to the fullest. Since they have ceased to be, all they are is a memory in the mind of God!

Many others will inhabit the earth during the Millennium also. These will be the unrighteous dead of all ages. They will be raised and given another chance to accept the rule of God. They too will have to be re-created according to God's memory. A final group making up the population will be the children born to Witnesses who survived the battle of Armageddon: "the Armageddon survivors will enjoy also the grand privilege of fulfilling a divine mandate to procreate."[17] The children will be born to life and will be tested. "Anyone who refuses to obey God's kingdom after a long-enough trial will be put to death."[18]

So almost everyone will get a second chance. Those destroyed at Armageddon, however, will not. They will have been annihilated forever. They had one chance, did not live up to it, and now will be cut off from life forever. At least in this there is some truth. The Bible, however, teaches that *all* men have only one chance: "It is appointed unto men *once* to die, but after this the judgment" (Heb. 9:27).

The Purpose of the Millennium. There will be a two-fold purpose of the Millennium, according to the Witnesses. First, those in it will be put to work to transform it into a paradise like Eden. However, this "will not require the full thousand years of Christ's reign"[19] (or perhaps, more accurately, Michael's reign).

Second, the Millennium will be set up to give sinners a second chance. "An extensive educational work will therefore be necessary in the course of the thousand-year reign when millions of 'unrighteous' dead, needing instruction in God's law, are scheduled to arise from their tombs."[20]

The Conditions During the Millennium. During the Millennium the earth will develop into a global paradise. The problem of the pollution of nature will be rectified.[21] There will be an endless variety of plant and animal life and much to see:

> You might enjoy visiting a rocky or sandy coastline unmarred by garbage or industrial pollutants. There you could listen to the waves and watch graceful gulls and other sea life. Inland you would find a variety of forests, each with its distinctive animals and plants, and all free of the effects of ruinous exploitation by greedy men.[22]

The article goes on to talk about lofty snow-capped mountains and gentle slopes where there will be no beer cans or other litter. It also describes semi-arid plains: instead of these being man-made dust bowls, they will display their own natural vegetation and will abound with animals, large and small, wild and domestic.[23] In this state of affairs, those in the Millennium will draw peace and satisfaction from undisturbed nature.

The Capital of the Millennium. The Witnesses believe that the capital of the Millennium will be the New Jerusalem. To them the New Jerusalem is not a city with precious stones as its foundation, such as is described in Revelation 21:10–27. Instead, the Watchtower teaches that the New Jerusalem is only symbolic, that the "city" is the 144,000 who rule with Christ: "We can be sure that this symbolic 'city,' by the light of which the nations will walk, will render justice to all under its rule."[24]

The Climax of the Millennium. At the end of the thousand years Satan will be released from his "deathlike state." He will seek to usurp Jehovah's position as universal sovereign once more. He will "endeavor to turn all perfected mankind against God."[25] Though perfected, some will follow him. This endeavor of Satan's is the final test to prove the integrity of those in the Millennium. So it is possible that a person could be a faithful, hard-working Jehovah's Witness all through this life, survive the battle of Armageddon, serve Jehovah 998 years of the Millennium, then fall to Satan's guile, fail the last test and lose out at the very end. Salvation is not necessarily forever.

The Destruction of Satan

As we said, there will be those who follow Satan in his final challenge to the authority and sovereignty of God. But it will be to no avail, for Satan will be overthrown and cast into the Lake of Fire and Sulphur. This will be his second death.

Although Satan will be cast into the Lake of Fire, the Watchtower does not believe that he will spend eternity in everlasting torment. Rather, he will be drowned in everlasting destruction. He will be annihilated. "The ultimate end of Satan is complete annihilation."[26]

If we were to ask, "Does not Matthew 25:41 teach that there is an everlasting fire prepared for the devil and his angels?" the answer the Witnesses like to give is that this means he is preserved nowhere but is everlastingly consumed. He simply will no longer exist. "Satan will be dead!"[27] Even the New World Translation of Revelation 20:10 cannot convince them that Satan "shall be tormented day and night for ever and ever."

Eternity without End

Following the destruction of Satan comes the inauguration of the eternal ages. Eternity will be different for three groups of people: the wicked, the 144,000 and the Great Crowd.

Eternity for the Wicked. Actually, it is not correct to speak of an eternity for the wicked in Witness theology, for the Witnesses believe the wicked will not have an eternity. At different stages throughout time, some have already forever ceased to exist in any form. The first such wicked one was Adam. Cain was another early member of this group. The people of Noah's day, Judas Iscariot and the people living at the time of Armageddon who are not Jehovah's Witnesses will also be part of this number. Others of the group will be those of the Evil Slave class—Jehovah's Witnesses who left the fold. The final contingent will consist of the ones who follow Satan at the end of the Millennium.

By the time the Millennium comes to its end, most of the wicked will already have ceased to be. The Millennium rebels will then be cast into the Lake of Fire along with Satan at the close of that final rebellion. Again, this does not mean an eternity in torment. It means that they will be disintegrated as if they had never existed at all.

The denial of hell was one of the earliest dogmas of Russellism and has remained a cardinal point in Witness theology ever since. Hell is called a "God-dishonoring doctrine."[28] The book *Let God Be True* has a chapter entitled, "Hell, a Place of Rest in Hope."[29] In this chapter the doctrine of hell is rejected on the following grounds:

1. It is stated that hell refers only to man's com-

mon grave. This is a half-truth—the Hebrew word *sheol* can mean either the grave *or* hell. One must consider the context to see which it refers to in a given text. The texts speaking of hell never refer simply to the grave.

2. It is stated that Gehenna refers to a garbage dump outside of Jerusalem. This is another half-truth. There was a garbage dump there, but Christ was not referring to the dump when He described Gehenna as a place of the lost.

3. It is stated that Christendom teaches that Satan and the demons are down in hell keeping the fires going and otherwise making things difficult for the people there, whereas the Bible shows Satan to be free until the battle of Armageddon has ended. This view is based on fantasy—Bible-believing Christians do not hold that Satan is hell's fire-stoker! Christians hold that he is free until the end of the Tribulation, then is bound for a thousand years, is freed for a brief time and finally is cast into the Lake of Fire after the Millennium is over. He will be tormented in the flame and will wish that it would die out!

4. It is stated that Jonah got out of hell. Not so! Jonah 2:2 is a verse where sheol should be translated grave: "From the depths of the grave I called for help" (Jonah 2:2, NIV).

5. It is stated that the account of the rich man and Lazarus is only a parable, and that this parable has been in the process of being fulfilled since 1919. But this is *not* a parable. Jesus never used names of people in His parables. This is a real account and took place in Christ's time.

6. It is stated that the doctrine of hell originated with Satan, a statement the Watchtower likes to

make about a number of doctrines it finds distasteful.

7. It is stated that the existence of hell would mean that the soul would have to be immortal and indestructible. Exactly so!

8. It is stated that the doctrine of hell is unreasonable. It is not unreasonable at all. The wages of sin is death; sin must be punished. Jesus talked more about hell than He did about Heaven. Certainly we should not say that He was being unreasonable.

9. The doctrine of hell is pictured as contrary to God's love. It is not. God is both a holy God and a God of love. He loved the world so much He sent His only begotten Son into the world to die on a cross to pay the penalty for sin. Those who refuse to accept the offered pardon have no one to blame but themselves. God's holiness and justice demand that sin be punished.

10. It is stated that the doctrine of hell is repugnant to justice. Not at all. For God to let sin go unpunished would be repugnant to justice. It would show that Jehovah is too weak to do anything about those who rebel against Him.

11. It is stated that hell is wholly unscriptural. Nothing could be farther from the truth. Matthew 25:46 says, "These shall go away into *everlasting* punishment: but the righteous into life *eternal*." The words "everlasting" and "eternal" are absolutely identical in Greek—*aionion*. The Bible declares that both punishment and life are eternal. Likewise Hebrews 6:2 speaks of "eternal judgment" ("everlasting judgment," NWT) and again the word is *aionion*. First Timothy 1:17 uses this

same word of Jehovah God: "Now unto the King *eternal,* immortal, invisible, the only wise God. . . ." Thus, it is senseless on the one hand to say that the Bible says nothing about hell and on the other hand to say that hell is not eternal. Is everlasting life not eternal? Is Jehovah God not eternal?

Moreover, Revelation 14:11 says, "the smoke of their torment ascendeth up *for ever and ever.* . . ." Revelation 15:7 describes "the wrath of God, who liveth *for ever and ever.*" "For ever and ever" comes from the same Greek phrase in both cases. Certainly Jehovah will live forever; so ultimate punishment must also be forever.

There can be no doubt that the Bible teaches eternal punishment. Read John 5:29 and Revelation 20:10 and 15. For the Watchtower to say hell is unscriptural is like an ostrich sticking its head in the sand.

Eternity for the 144,000. The Watchtower teaches that the Jehovah's Witnesses who make up the 144,000 will spend eternity with Christ in Heaven. They were given immortality at the time of their resurrection to spirit life. "The 144,000 remain in heaven throughout eternity; they never come down again to inhabit the earth."[30] They will reign with Christ forever in God's theocracy, bringing blessings to those on earth. Jehovah will be the supreme Sovereign.

Eternity for the Great Crowd. The Great Crowd will not have the privilege of going to Heaven. They will spend eternity down here: "They attain to eternal life on earth."[31] Not only do they not attain Heaven, they do not attain immortality either. Neither is eternal life their true portion, for they must keep eating food to sustain life.[32]

The Witnesses take great pains to try to refute the belief in the destruction of the present earth when the new heavens and the new earth are to be established.[33] For if the present earth were destroyed, the eternal earthly paradise concept would be jeopardized. Thus, the heavens which shall pass away are held not to be real heavens at all, but are human governments.[34] The earth that passes away in turn is not this planet, but wicked men. Therefore:

> The passing away of the symbolic heavens and the destruction of ungodly mankind will pave the way for making our earthly planet a most delightful home for those seeking to do God's will.[35]

It is said that the paradise earth will be the home of billions. Those on earth will continue to have children until it becomes full. At that time they will have no more children. Since no one will die the earth will reach a saturation point and no more will be born.

> Then, in the righteous world, the Almighty by means of his kingdom will shower down upon earth's billions of perfect, loyal inhabitants an overflow of divine blessings that will fill their hearts with everlasting gladness. Here will be a world without Adamic death, illness, sorrow, tears, or religious confusion. A secure world it will be, worshipping Jehovah and filled with love and joy and all things desirable. It will remain, not for a thousand,

or a million, or even a thousand-million years, but forever.[36]

Such is the eternity the present Jehovah's Witness can expect. On the surface it might seem delightful. However, it will mean missing Heaven. It will mean not having a truly glorified body but always being dependent on food. It will mean not being present forever with the Lord. Although there are to be no more tears, the whole concept is very sad indeed.

"Let us hear the conclusion of the whole matter."
Ecclesiastes 12:13a

15

IN A NUTSHELL

WE have seen in our study that in every single area of systematic theology Jehovah's Witnesses differ radically from orthodox Christianity. In bibliology, although the Witnesses believe in verbal plenary inspiration,[1] they often nullify the benefits of such a view by a fantastically allegorical system of interpretation. In theology proper the doctrine of the Trinity is denied as well as the omnipresence of God.

In Christology, Christ's *eternal* preexistence is denied, as is His deity. It is taught that His humanity ceased at the cross. His unity with the Father, His bodily resurrection, His physical ascension and His visible, physical return all are denied.

In pneumatology, the doctrine of the Spirit, the personality of the Spirit is denied and the work of the Spirit is minimized. In angelology the Witnesses teach that Christ in both His preexistent and post-earthly states is none other than the angel Michael.

In Satanology we are told that Satan, as well as the demons, will be annihilated. In anthropology, the doctrine of man, we find that man does not possess a soul but *is* a soul, and man's spirit is no more than an activating principle. In hamartiology, the doctrine of sin, we are told that man can be saved from sin by the ransom of One Who was only human, nothing more.

In soteriology, the doctrine of salvation, eternal security is denied. The Witnesses teach that there are two ways of salvation. The 144,000, the anointed class, may seek and receive the born-again experience. The vast majority of mankind does not need to be born again and, in fact, cannot be. In ecclesiology, the doctrine of the church, there is only one true congregation of God and that is the Jehovah's Witnesses.

In eschatology, the doctrine of last things, it is said that Christ's second advent took place in 1914 and was invisible and spiritual. The kingdom of heaven has already been established and Satan has already been cast out of Heaven. The battle of Armageddon was to have taken place by the fall of 1975. The Millennium will give the unrighteous dead a second chance for salvation. At the close of the Millennium Satan will be annihilated. The wicked will be annihilated for eternity. Only 144,000 individuals (Jehovah's Witnesses, naturally) will be in Heaven, having gotten there by sacrificing their right to an earthly life, so they earn their own way. The remainder of mankind will spend eternity on earth and will never get to Heaven.

The Witnesses, then, do not simply promote a few unique interpretations in minor areas of doctrine. Their whole system is permeated with heresy from beginning to end.

PART III

The Witness of God

THE WITNESS OF GOD

"IF we receive the witness of men, the witness of God is greater: for this is the witness of God which he hath testified of his Son.

"He that believeth on the Son of God hath the witness in himself: he that believeth not God hath made him a liar; because he believeth not the record that God gave of his Son.

"And this is the record, that God hath given to us eternal life, and this life is in his Son.

"He that hath the Son hath life; and he that hath not the Son of God hath not life.

"These things have I written unto you that believe on the name of the Son of God; that ye may know that ye have eternal life, and that ye may believe on the name of the Son of God" (1 John 5:9–13).

* * * * * * * * * * * * * * * * *

"But as many as received him, to them gave

he power to become the sons of God, even to them that believe on his name" (John 1:12).

* * * * * * * * * * * * * * * * *

"For by grace are ye saved through faith; and that not of yourselves: it is the gift of God:

"Not of works, lest any man should boast" (Eph. 2:8, 9).

APPENDIX

Other Members of the Russellite Family

Eleven religious groups besides the Jehovah's Witnesses have sprung up from the teachings of Charles Taze Russell.[1] Some of these groups hold more closely to Russell's views than do the current Jehovah's Witnesses. Some of them have names that make them sound Biblical. They are listed here to alert the reader that they are branches of the same tree as the Witnesses. The two largest are the Laymen's Home Missionary Movement and the Dawn Bible Students Association. The eleven—along with their corresponding periodicals—are:

1. Back to the Bible Way, Fort Lauderdale, Florida. Publishes *Back to the Bible Way*.

2. Christian Believers Conference, Cicero, Illinois. Publishes *The Kingdom Scribe* and *The Berean*.

3. Christian Bible Students Association, Warren, Michigan. Publishes *Harvest Message*.

4. Dawn Bible Students Association, East Rutherford, New Jersey. Publishes *The Dawn*.

5. Epiphany Bible Students Association, Mt. Dora, Florida. Publishes a monthly newsletter.

6. Laodicean Home Missionary Movement, Levittown, Pennsylvania. Publishes *The Present Truth of the Apocalypsis*.

7. Laymen's Home Missionary Movement, Philadelphia, Pennsylvania. Publishes *The Bible Standard and Herald of Christ's Kingdom*.

8. New Creation Bible Students, Hartford, Connecticut. Publishes *The New Creation*.

9. Pastoral Bible Institute, St. Louis, Missouri. This is an agency for the Associated Bible Students. Publishes *The Herald of Christ's Kingdom*.

10. Philanthropic Assembly, North Bergen, New Jersey. Publishes *The Monitor of the Reign of Justice*.

11. Western Bible Students Association, Seattle, Washington. No publication.

NOTES ON SOURCES

Chapter 1

[1]Marley Cole, *Jehovah's Witnesses* (New York: Vantage Press, 1955), 17.

[2]Gordon R. Lewis, *Confronting the Cults* (Philadelphia: Presbyterian and Reformed Publishing Co., 1966), 16.

[3]Thus Phelan wrote in 1927, "Since Russell's death, in 1916, the movement seems to be losing ground." M. Phelan, comp., *Handbook of All Denominations* (Nashville: Cokesbury Press, 1927), 142.

[4]Edmond Charles Gruss, *Cults and the Occult in the Age of Aquarius* (Nutley, N J: Presbyterian and Reformed Publishing Co., 1972), 8.

[5]Anthony A. Hoekema, *The Four Major Cults* (Grand Rapids: Wm. B. Eerdmans Publishing Co., 1963), 234.

[6]Walter R. Martin and Norman H. Klann, *Jehovah of the Watchtower*, revised and updated (Chicago: Moody Press, 1974), 14.

Chapter 2

[1]Walter R. Martin, *The Kingdom of the Cults: An Analysis of the Major Cult Systems in the Present Christian Era,* rev. ed. (Minneapolis: Bethany Fellowship, 1968), 34.

[2]Hoekema, *Four Major Cults,* 223.

[3]J. Gordon Melton, *The Encyclopedia of American Religions,* 2 vols. (Wilmington, NC: McGrath Publishing Co., 1978), 1:461.

[4]*History of the Advent Message* cited by Harold J. Berry in *Examining the Cults* (Lincoln, NE: Back to the Bible, 1979), 101.

[5]Melton, *Encyclopedia of American Religions,* 1:481.

[6]Edmond Charles Gruss, *Apostles of Denial: An Examination and Exposé of the History, Doctrines and Claims of the Jehovah's Witnesses* (Philadelphia: Presbyterian and Reformed Publishing Co., 1970), 39.

[7]Hoekema, *Four Major Cults,* 224.

[8]See, for example, *Then Is Finished the Mystery of God* (Brooklyn: Watchtower Bible and Tract Society, 1969), 58.

[9]See "Why Such a Costly Ransom Price?" *The Watchtower* (July 15, 1975): 429–32.

[10]Gruss, *Apostles of Denial,* 44.

[11]Jan Karel Van Baalen, *The Chaos of Cults: A Study in Present-Day Isms* (Grand Rapids: Wm. B. Eerdmans Publishing Co., 1965), 233.

[12]Ibid.

[13]Gruss, *Apostles of Denial,* 45.

[14]Melton, *Encyclopedia of American Religions,* 1:483.

[15]Martin, *Kingdom of the Cults,* 40.

[16]Joe Hewitt, *I Was Raised a Jehovah's Witness:*

The True Story of a Former J. W. (Denver: Accent Books, 1979), 8.

17Gruss, *Cults and the Occult,* 8.

Chapter 3

1Hoekema, *Four Major Cults,* 228.

2Gruss, *Apostles of Denial,* 53.

3Ibid., 55.

4*Then Is Finished the Mystery of God,* 112.

5Hoekema, *Four Major Cults,* 229.

6Martin and Klann, *Jehovah of the Watchtower,* 26.

7Frank S. Mead, *Handbook of Denominations in the United States* (New York: Abingdon-Cokesbury Press, 1951), 100–101.

8Martin and Klann, *Jehovah of the Watchtower,* 27.

9Royston Pike, *Jehovah's Witnesses* (London: Watts and Co., 1954), 21.

10William J. Schnell, *Thirty Years a Watch Tower Slave: The Confessions of a Converted Jehovah's Witness* (Grand Rapids: Baker Book House, 1956), 41.

11Gruss, *Apostles of Denial,* 57.

12Walter R. Martin, *The Rise of the Cults* (Grand Rapids: Zondervan Publishing House, 1955), 22.

13*Let God Be True,* rev. ed. (Brooklyn: Watchtower Bible and Tract Society, Inc., 1952), 37 (page 40 in original edition).

14Gruss, *Apostles of Denial,* 65.

Chapter 4

1Constant H. Jacquet, Jr., ed., *Yearbook of American and Canadian Churches, 1973* (New York: Abingdon Press, 1973), 64.

[2]Hoekema, *Four Major Cults,* 231.

[3]Gruss, *Apostles of Denial,* 67.

[4]Chandler W. Sterling, *The Witnesses: One God, One Victory* (Chicago: Henry Regnery Company, 1975), 65.

[5]Arnold Black Rhodes, ed., *The Church Faces the Isms* (New York: Abindgon Press, 1958), 82.

[6]Sterling, *The Witnesses,* 64.

[7]Irvine Robertson, *What the Cults Believe* (Chicago: Moody Press, 1966), 48.

[8]Sterling, *The Witnesses,* 74.

[9]Hewitt, *I Was Raised a Jehovah's Witness,* 91.

Chapter 5

[1]See Alan Rogerson, *Millions Now Living Will Never Die* (London: Constable & Co., 1969), 76.

[2]*Make Sure of All Things, Hold Fast to What Is Fine* (Brooklyn: Watchtower Bible and Tract Society of New York, Inc., 1965), 45.

[3]Ibid.

[4]Ibid.

[5]Ibid., 49.

[6]Ibid., 50.

[7]Ibid., 51.

[8]Ibid.

[9]Ibid., 53.

[10]Ibid., 52.

[11]*Let God Be True,* 43.

[12]*Is the Bible Really the Word of God?* (Brooklyn: Watchtower Bible and Tract Society of New York, Inc., 1969), 151.

[13]*Let God Be True,* 18–19 (p. 20 in original edition).

[14]*Then Is Finished the Mystery of God,* 264.

[15]Ibid., 271.

[16]Ibid., 277.

[17]Ibid.

[18]*Make Sure of All Things,* 53–54.

[19]Anthony A. Hoekema, *Jehovah's Witnesses* (Exeter, Eng.: The Paternoster Press, 1973), 26.

[20]See James W. Sire, *Scripture Twisting* (Downers Grove, IL: InterVarsity Press, 1980), 80–82. This is an excellent book on the ways cults in general misuse the Scriptures.

[21]Sterling, *The Witnesses,* 65.

[22]Hoekema, *Jehovah's Witnesses,* 26.

[23]Robert H. Countess, *The Jehovah's Witnesses' New Testament: A Critical Analysis of the New World Translation of the Christian Greek Scriptures* (Phillipsburg, NJ: Presbyterian and Reformed Publishing Co., 1982).

[24]Gordon R. Lewis, *The Bible, the Christian and Jehovah's Witnesses* (Phillipsburg, NJ: Presbyterian and Reformed Publishing Co., 1966).

Chapter 6

[1]*Things in Which It Is Impossible for God to Lie* (Brooklyn: Watchtower Bible and Tract Society of New York, Inc., 1965), 9, citing *The Encyclopedia Americana* (1956), 12:743.

[2]*Things in Which,* 15.

[3]Ibid., 12.

[4]Ibid., 13.

[5]Ibid., 17.

[6]*Let God Be True,* 25 (p. 27 in original edition).

[7]*Make Sure . . . Hold Fast,* 266.

[8]*Let God Be True,* 25 (p. 27 in original edition).

[9]*The Truth That Leads to Eternal Life* (Brooklyn: Watchtower Bible and Tract Society of New York, Inc., 1968), 19.

[10]*Let God Be True,* 25–26.

[11] *Make Sure of All Things* (Brooklyn: Watchtower Bible and Tract Society, 1953), 188.

[12] Hoekema, *Four Major Cults,* 256.

[13] *Things in Which,* 259.

[14] Ibid., 254–69.

[15] *Make Sure . . . Hold Fast,* 486.

[16] *Let God Be True,* 107 (p. 88 in original edition).

[17] Ibid., 105 (p. 86 in original edition).

[18] Ibid., 108 (p. 89 in original edition).

[19] Charles T. Russell, *The Unfinished Mystery,* cited by William J. Whalen in *Armageddon around the Corner: A Report on Jehovah's Witnesses* (New York: The John Day Company, 1962), 83.

[20] *Let God Be True,* 101 (p. 82 in original edition).

[21] Ibid.

[22] Ibid., 102 (pp. 83–84 in original edition).

[23] Ibid., 109 (p. 91 in original edition).

[24] *Things in Which,* 256.

[25] *Let God Be True,* 111; *The Truth That Leads,* 22; *Things in Which,* 256.

[26] *The Truth That Leads,* 24.

[27] *Make Sure . . . Hold Fast,* 488.

[28] Ibid., 216.

[29] Ibid., 282.

[30] Ibid., 215.

[31] Gruss, *Apostles of Denial,* 81.

[32] *Things in Which,* 22–23.

[33] Gruss, *Apostles of Denial,* 81.

[34] *Let God Be True,* 28.

[35] "Aid to Bible Understanding," *The Watchtower* (November 1, 1975): 665.

[36] *Things in Which,* 263.

[37] *Make Sure . . . Hold Fast,* 267.

[38] Robertson, *What the Cults Believe,* 50.

[39] *Let God Be True,* 24.

[40] *The Truth That Leads,* 19.

[41] *Make Sure . . . Hold Fast,* 486.

[42] Ibid., 487.

[43] Gruss, *Apostles of Denial,* 81.

[44] *Let God Be True,* 25.

[45] *Make Sure . . . Hold Fast,* 288.

[46] Gruss, *Apostles of Denial,* 81.

[47] *The Truth That Leads,* 21.

[48] *Let God Be True,* 106.

[49] *The Truth That Leads,* 21.

[50] Ibid.

[51] *Did Man Get Here by Evolution or by Creation?* (Brooklyn: Watchtower Bible & Tract Society of New York, Inc., 1967), 152.

[52] Ibid., 158.

[53] *Make Sure . . . Hold Fast,* 282.

[54] Ibid.

[55] *Things in Which,* 18.

[56] *Make Sure . . . Hold Fast,* 132.

[57] Ibid.

[58] Ibid., 134.

[59] *Equipped for Every Good Work* (Brooklyn: Watchtower Bible and Tract Society, 1946), 64.

[60] *Let God Be True,* 29.

[61] Ibid., 37–38.

[62] Mead, *Handbook of Denominations,* 101.

Chapter 7

[1] Lewis, *Confronting the Cults,* 23.

[2] Charles Caldwell Ryrie, *A Survey of Bible Doctrine* (Chicago: Moody Press, 1972), 51–52.

[3] *From Paradise Lost to Paradise Regained* (Brooklyn: Watchtower Bible and Tract Society of New York, Inc., 1958), 127.

[4]Ibid., 122.

[5]Ibid., 123.

[6]See *The Kingdom Is at Hand* (Brooklyn: Watchtower Bible and Tract Society, 1944), 49.

[7]Hoekema, *Jehovah's Witnesses*, 63.

[8]*Make Sure . . . Hold Fast*, 485.

[9]*New World Translation of the Holy Scriptures*, rev. ed. (Brooklyn: Watchtower Bible and Tract Society of New York, Inc., 1961), 1151.

[10]*Things in Which*, 123.

[11]*Let God Be True*, 34.

[12]Ibid., 36.

[13]*From Paradise Lost*, 127.

[14]*Let God Be True*, 37–38.

[15]*Did Man Get Here by Evolution?* 157.

[16]"What the Churches Do Not Tell You," *The Watchtower* (June 15, 1975): 357.

[17]"Why Such A Costly Ransom Price?" *The Watchtower* (July 15, 1975): 430.

[18]Ibid., 430–31.

[19]Ibid., 431.

[20]*Let God Be True*, 1946 ed., 101.

[21]Charles Taze Russell, *The Time Is at Hand*, vol. 2 of *Studies in the Scriptures* (Brooklyn: Watchtower Bible and Tract Society, 1912–1917), 129.

[22]Joseph F. Rutherford, *The Harp of God* (Brooklyn: Watchtower Bible and Tract Society, 1921), 173.

[23]*The Truth Shall Make You Free* (Brooklyn: Watchtower Bible and Tract Society, Inc., 1943), 264.

[24]See Elmer T. Clark, *The Small Sects in America* (New York: Abingdon-Cokesbury Press, 1949), 46.

[25] *Let God Be True*, 273.
[26] Ibid., 40.
[27] Ibid., 41.
[28] Ibid.
[29] *Things in Which*, 264.
[30] *Jehovah's Witnesses in the Divine Purpose* (Brooklyn: Watchtower Bible and Tract Society of Pennsylvania, Inc., 1959), 18.
[31] Whalen, *Armageddon around the Corner*, 216.
[32] See, for example, the dating method in *Holy Spirit: the Force Behind the Coming New Order* (Brooklyn: Watchtower Bible and Tract Society of New York, Inc., 1976), 30, 164.

Chapter 8

[1] *Things in Which*, 169.
[2] *The Truth That Leads*, 24.
[3] Ryrie, *Survey of Bible Doctrine*, 68–69.
[4] *Make Sure . . . Hold Fast*, 153.
[5] *This Means Everlasting Life* (Brooklyn: Watchtower Bible and Tract Society, Inc., 1950), 165.
[6] *Holy Spirit: The Force Behind the Coming New Order* (Brooklyn: Watchtower Bible and Tract Society of New York, Inc., 1976), 11.
[7] *This Means Everlasting Life*, 166.
[8] *Make Sure . . . Hold Fast*, 467.
[9] *Holy Spirit: The Force*, 157.
[10] *This Means Everlasting Life*, 169.
[11] Ibid., 171.
[12] *Holy Spirit: The Force*, 181.

Chapter 9

[1] *Things in Which*, 120.
[2] *Make Sure . . . Hold Fast*, 288.
[3] Ibid., 132.
[4] *Things in Which*, 128.

[5]Ibid., 131.
[6]Ibid., 127.
[7]*Make Sure . . . Hold Fast,* 9.
[8]*Things in Which,* 129.
[9]*Make Sure . . . Hold Fast,* 10–13.
[10]*This Means Everlasting Life,* 34.
[11]*Let God Be True,* rev. ed., 57.
[12]Ibid.
[13]Ibid., 57–58.
[14]*Did Man Get Here by Evolution?* 151.
[15]*The Truth That Leads,* 56.
[16]*Let God Be True,* 60.
[17]Gruss, *Apostles of Denial,* 84.
[18]*Let God Be True,* 59.
[19]Ibid.
[20]*From Paradise Lost,* 34.
[21]*Let God Be True,* 59.
[22]Ibid., 62.
[23]*Make Sure . . . Hold Fast,* 157.
[24]*Let God Be True,* 63.
[25]Ibid., 65.
[26]Ibid., 64.
[27]Whalen, *Armageddon around the Corner,* 85.
[28]*The Truth That Leads,* 58–59.
[29]*Things in Which,* 169.
[30]Ibid.

Chapter 10

[1]*Did Man Get Here by Evolution?* 1–130.
[2]Edmond C. Gruss, *The Jehovah's Witnesses and
    Prophetic Speculation* (Nutley, NJ: Presbyte-
    rian and Reformed Publishing Co., 1972), 114.
[3]Hoekema, *Four Major Cults,* 266.
[4]*Make Sure of All Things,* 349.
[5]"What Is the Bible's View? What Is the Soul?"

Awake! (August 8, 1975): 28. See also "Your 'Soul' Is You", Chapter 5 of *Things in Which It Is Impossible for God to Lie.*

6"What Is the Bible's View?" 27.

7*Let God Be True,* 68.

8*New World Translation,* 9.

9"Your Soul," *The Watchtower* (December 15, 1975): 744.

10F. W. Thomas, *Masters of Deception: A Christian Analysis of the Anti-Biblical Teachings of the Jehovah's Witnesses* (Grand Rapids: Baker Book House, n. d.), p. 99.

11Gruss, *Apostles of Denial,* 157.

12*Let God Be True,* 74.

13Clark, *The Small Sects in America,* 46.

14*Let God Be True,* 74.

15Ibid., 145.

16Ibid., 74.

17*From Paradise Lost,* 35.

18"Paradise—A Desirable Place in Which to Live," *Awake!* (December 22, 1975): 3.

19*Let God Be True,* 74.

Chapter 11

1Mary Baker Eddy, *Science and Health with Key to the Scriptures* (Boston: Trustees of Mary Baker Eddy, 1910), 475.

2"Our Refuge under the Incorruptible 'Kingdom of the Heavens'," *The Watchtower* (November 15, 1975): 685.

3"Increasing Crime and Violence," *Awake!* (October 22, 1979): 4.

4*Make Sure . . . Hold Fast,* 458.

5*Let God Be True,* 119.

Chapter 12

[1] *Make Sure . . . Hold Fast*, 438.
[2] *Let God Be True*, 114.
[3] Ibid., 116.
[4] Ibid., 119.
[5] *Make Sure . . . Hold Fast*, 440.
[6] *Let God Be True*, 295.
[7] Ibid., 295-6.
[8] Gruss, *Apostles of Denial*, 150.
[9] *Let God Be True*, 302-3.
[10] Hoekema, *Four Major Cults*, 283.
[11] *You May Survive Armageddon into God's New World* (Brooklyn: Watchtower Bible and Tract Society, Inc., 1955), 181.
[12] Hoekema, *Four Major Cults*, 284.
[13] *Let God Be True*, 231.
[14] *Make Sure . . . Hold Fast*, 439.
[15] *Let God Be True*, 132.
[16] Ibid., 298.

Chapter 13

[1] James E. Talmadge, *The Articles of Faith*, 5th ed. (Salt Lake City: 1909), 33-38.
[2] Connie M. Heidebrecht, "The Wierwille Way Trapped Me," *Escape from Darkness: Real Life Dramas by People Set Free from Soul-Shackling Cults and Religions*, comp. James R. Adair and Ted Miller (Wheaton, IL: Victor Books, 1982), 26.
[3] Herbert W. Armstrong, "Personal from Herbert W. Armstrong," *The Plain Truth* (July-August, 1973), cited by Harold J. Berry, *Examining the Cults* (Lincoln, NE: Back to the Bible, 1979), 9.

[4] *From Paradise Lost*, 193.

[5] Joseph F. Rutherford, *Enemies* (Brooklyn: Watchtower Bible and Tract Society, 1937), 63.

[6] Joseph F. Rutherford, *Reconciliation* (Brooklyn: Watchtower Bible and Tract Society, 1928), 85.

[7] "The Death of a God," *The Watchtower* (May 1, 1975): 269.

[8] *The Truth That Leads*, 120.

[9] Ibid., 115.

[10] Ibid., 120.

[11] Ibid., 121.

[12] *The Watchtower*, July 1, 1963, 411–12, cited by W. C. Stevenson in *The Inside Story of Jehovah's Witnesses* (New York: Hart Publishing Co., Inc., 1968), 174.

[13] *Inside Story*, 174.

[14] Ted Dencher, *Why I Left Jehovah's Witnesses* (Fort Washington, PA: Christian Literature Crusade, 1980), 45.

[15] See William J. Whalen, *Armageddon around the Corner*, 85.

[16] See the number 14 above, plus the following testimonies of former Jehovah's Witnesses: William J. Schnell, *Thirty Years A Watch Tower Slave: The Confessions of a Converted Jehovah's Witness*; Joe Hewitt, *I Was Raised A Jehovah's Witness: The True Story of a Former J.W.*; William Cetnar, "I Was a False Witness," in *Escape from Darkness*; and Edmond C. Gruss, comp., *We Left Jehovah's Witnesses, A Non-Prophet Organization; with the Testimonies of Converted Jehovah's Witnesses*, (Phillipsburg, NJ: Presbyterian and Reformed

Publishing Co., 1974). See also W. C. Stevenson, *The Inside Story of Jehovah's Witnesses* (New York: Hart Publishing Co., Inc., 1968).

[17] *Let God Be True*, 297–8.

Chapter 14

[1] Clark, *The Small Sects in America*, 46.

[2] "Paradise—a Desirable Place in Which to Live," *Awake!* (December 22, 1975): 3. "A Global Paradise—Why Possible?" Ibid., 4–8. "Will *You* See All the Earth Become a Paradise?" Ibid., 8–12.

[3] *This Means Everlasting Life*, 215.

[4] Ibid.

[5] Ibid., 220.

[6] Van Baalen, *Chaos of Cults*, 208–9.

[7] *Let God Be True*, 125–6.

[8] Ibid., 277.

[9] *From Paradise Lost*, 205.

[10] Herbert H. Stroup, *The Jehovah's Witnesses* (New York: Columbia University Press, 1945), 55.

[11] Joseph F. Rutherford, *Children* (Brooklyn: Watchtower Bible and Tract Society, Inc., 1941), n.p.

[12] "The One Government for One World under God's Sovereignty," *The Watchtower* (October 15, 1975): 622.

[13] *From Paradise Lost*, 204.

[14] Ibid.

[15] *The Truth That Leads*, 97–100.

[16] *From Paradise Lost*, 211.

[17] *Let God Be True*, 268.

[18] *From Paradise Lost*, 237.

[19] *Let God Be True*, 270.

[20]Ibid.

[21]"Is Pollution God's Fault?" *Awake!* (July 8, 1975): 11.

[22]"Paradise—a Desirable Place," 3.

[23]Ibid.

[24]"A Capital for the Universe," *The Watchtower* (August 15, 1975): 492.

[25]*Let God Be True*, 270.

[26]Ibid., 64.

[27]Ibid., 65.

[28]Ibid., 88.

[29]Ibid., 88–99.

[30]Hoekema, *Four Major Cults*, 325.

[31]*This Means Everlasting Life*, 238.

[32]Hoekema, *Four Major Cults*, 324.

[33]"A Book of Myths or a Misrepresented Guide?" *Awake!* (October 8, 1975): 11.

[34]"What Is the Bible's View? Will the Earth One Day Be Destroyed?" *Awake!* (August 22, 1975): 28.

[35]Ibid.

[36]*Let God Be True*, 270-1.

Chapter 15
[1]Gruss, *Apostles of Denial*, 79.

Appendix
[1]Melton, *Encyclopedia of American Religions*, 1:481-93.

BIBLIOGRAPHY

General Books

Berry, Harold J. *Examining the Cults.* Lincoln, NE: Back to the Bible, 1979.

Bjornstad, James. *Counterfeits at Your Door.* Glendale, CA: Regal Books, 1979.

Breese, Dave. *Know the Marks of Cults.* Wheaton, IL: Victor Books, 1975.

Cetnar, William. "I Was A False Witness." In *Escape From Darkness*, compiled by James R. Adair and Ted Miller, 31–37. Wheaton, IL: Victor Books, 1982.

Clark, Elmer T. *The Small Sects in America.* New York: Abingdon-Cokesbury Press, 1949.

Cole, Marley. *Jehovah's Witnesses.* New York: Vantage Press, 1955.

_____ . *Triumphant Kingdom.* New York: Criterion Books, 1957.

Countess, Robert H. *The Jehovah's Witnesses' New Testament: A Critical Analysis of the New*

World Translation of the Christian Greek Scriptures. Phillipsburg, NJ: Presbyterian and Reformed Publishing Co., 1982.

Dencher, Ted. *The Watchtower Heresy versus the Bible.* Chicago: Moody Press, 1961.

—————. *Why I Left Jehovah's Witnesses.* Rev. ed. Fort Washington, PA: Christian Literature Crusade, 1980.

Duncan, Homer. *Heart to Heart Talks with Jehovah's Witnesses.* Lubbock, TX: Missionary Crusader, n.d.

Eddy, Mary Baker. *Science and Health with Key to the Scripture.* Boston: Trustees of Mary Baker Eddy, 1910.

Forrest, E. R. *Errors of Russellism.* Anderson, IN: Gospel Trumpet Co., 1915.

Gerstner, John H. *The Theology of the Major Sects.* Grand Rapids: Baker Book House, 1960.

Gruss, Edmond Charles. *Apostles of Denial: An Examination and Exposé of the History, Doctrines and Claims of the Jehovah's Witnesses.* Philadelphia: Presbyterian and Reformed Publishing Co., 1970.

—————. *Cults and the Occult in the Age of Aquarius.* Nutley, NJ: Presbyterian and Reformed Publishing Co., 1972.

Gruss, Edmond Charles, comp. *We Left Jehovah's Witnesses, a Non-Prophet Organization.* Nutley, NJ: Presbyterian and Reformed Publishing Co., 1974.

Heidebrecht, Connie M. "The Wierwille Way Trapped Me." In *Escape From Darkness,* compiled by James R. Adair and Ted Miller, 22–30. Wheaton, IL: Victor Books, 1982.

Hewitt, Joe. *I Was Raised a Jehovah's Witness:*

The True Story of a Former J.W. Denver: Accent Books, 1979.

Hoekema, Anthony A. *The Four Major Cults.* Grand Rapids: Wm. B. Eerdmans Publishing Co., 1963.

————. *Jehovah's Witnesses.* Exeter, Eng.: The Paternoster Press, 1973.

Hudson, Winthrop S. *Religion in America.* 4th ed. New York: Macmillan Publishing Company, 1987.

Irvine, William C. *Heresies Exposed: A Brief Critical Examination in the Light of the Holy Scriptures of Some of the Prevailing Heresies and False Teachings of Today.* New York: Loizeaux Brothers, n.d.

Jacquet, Constant H., Jr., ed. *Yearbook of American and Canadian Churches.* New York: Abingdon Press, 1973.

Lewis, Gordon R. *The Bible, the Christian and Jehovah's Witnesses.* Phillipsburg, NJ: Presbyterian and Reformed Publishing Co., 1966.

————. *Confronting the Cults.* Philadelphia: Presbyterian and Reformed Publishing Co., 1966.

Martin, Walter R., and Norman H. Klann. *Jehovah of the Watchtower.* Rev. ed. Chicago: Moody Press, 1974.

Martin, Walter R. *Jehovah's Witnesses.* Minneapolis: Bethany Fellowship, 1957.

————. *The Kingdom of the Cults: An Analysis of the Major Systems in the Present Christian Era.* Rev. ed. Minneapolis: Bethany Fellowship, 1968.

————. *The Rise of the Cults.* Grand Rapids: Zondervan Publishing Co., 1955.

McKinney, George D., Jr. *The Theology of the Jehovah's Witnesses.* Grand Rapids: Zondervan Publishing House, 1962.

Mead, Frank S. *Handbook of Denominations in the United States.* New York: Abingdon-Cokesbury Press, 1951.

Melton, J. Gordon. *The Encyclopedia of American Religions.* 2 vols. Wilmington, NC: McGrath Publishing Co., 1978.

Morey, Robert A. *How to Answer a Jehovah's Witness.* Minneapolis: Bethany House Publishers, 1980.

Passantino, Robert and Gretchen. *Answers to the Cultist at Your Door.* Eugene, OR: Harvest House Publishers, 1981.

Phelan, M., comp. *Handbook of All Denominations.* Nashville: Cokesbury Press, 1927.

Pike, Royston. *Jehovah's Witnesses.* London: Watts and Co., 1954.

Rhodes, Arnold Black, ed. *The Church Faces the Isms.* New York: Abingdon Press, 1958.

Robertson, Irvine. *What the Cults Believe.* Chicago: Moody Press, 1966.

Rogerson, Alan. *Millions Now Living Will Never Die.* London: Constable & Co., 1969.

Ryrie, Charles Caldwell. *A Survey of Bible Doctrine.* Chicago: Moody Press, 1972.

Schnell, William J. *How to Witness to Jehovah's Witnesses.* Grand Rapids: Baker Book House, 1961.

————. *Into the Light of Christianity: the Basic Doctrines of the Jehovah's Witnesses in the Light of Scripture.* Grand Rapids: Baker Book House, 1959.

_____ . *Jehovah's Witnesses' Errors Exposed.* Grand Rapids: Baker Book House, 1959.

_____ . *Thirty Years a Watch Tower Slave: The Confessions of a Converted Jehovah's Witness.* Grand Rapids: Baker Book House, 1956.

Sire, James W. *Scripture Twisting: 20 Ways the Cults Misread the Bible.* Downers Grove, IL: InterVarsity Press, 1980.

Sterling, Chandler W. *The Witnesses: One God, One Victory.* Chicago: Henry Regnery Company, 1975.

Stevenson, W. C. *The Inside Story of Jehovah's Witnesses.* New York: Hart Publishing Co., 1967.

Stroup, Herbert H. *The Jehovah's Witnesses.* New York: Columbia University Press, 1945.

Talmadge, James E., *The Articles of Faith.* 5th ed. Salt Lake City, 1909.

Thomas, F. W. *Masters of Deception: A Christian Analysis of the Anti-Biblical Teachings of the Jehovah's Witnesses.* Grand Rapids: Baker Book House, n.d.

Van Baalen, Jan Karel. *The Chaos of Cults: A Study in Present-Day Isms.* 2d ed. Grand Rapids: Wm. B. Eerdmans Publishing Co., 1956.

Whalen, William J. *Armageddon around the Corner: A Report on Jehovah's Witnesses.* New York: The John Day Company, 1962.

The World Almanac and Book of Facts, 1987. New York: World Almanac, 1987.

Watchtower Books

The books listed in this category and the magazine articles in the next were all published by the Watchtower Bible and Tract Society and were used in preparation of this book. They are not endorsed for general reading.

Books by Charles Taze Russell
Russell, Charles Taze. *Studies in the Scriptures.* 7 vols. Brooklyn: Watchtower Bible and Tract Society, 1912–1917.

Books by Joseph F. Rutherford
Rutherford, Joseph F. *Children.* Brooklyn: Watchtower Bible and Tract Society, 1941.

————. *Creation.* Brooklyn: Watchtower Bible and Tract Society, 1927.

————. *Enemies.* Brooklyn: Watchtower Bible and Tract Society, 1937.

————. *Government.* Brooklyn: Watchtower Bible and Tract Society, 1928.

————. *The Harp of God.* Brooklyn: Watchtower Bible and Tract Society, 1921.

————. *Jehovah: The Revelation of the King of Eternity.* Brooklyn: Watchtower Bible and Tract Society, 1934.

————. *Life.* Brooklyn: Watchtower Bible and Tract Society, 1929.

————. *Light.* 2 vols. Brooklyn: Watchtower Bible and Tract Society, 1930.

————. *Preservation: The Explanation of Two Divinely Directed Prophetic Dramas Recorded in the Biblical Books of Esther and Ruth.* Brooklyn: Watchtower Bible and Tract Society, 1932.

————. *Reconciliation.* Brooklyn: Watchtower Bible and Tract Society, 1928.

————. *Salvation.* Brooklyn: Watchtower Bible and Tract Society, 1939.

————. *Vindication.* 3 vols. Brooklyn: Watchtower Bible and Tract Society, 1931.

Anonymous Watchtower Books

All Scripture Is Inspired of God and Beneficial. Brooklyn: Watchtower Bible and Tract Society of New York, Inc., 1963.

Babylon the Great Has Fallen! God's Kingdom Rules! Brooklyn: Watchtower Bible and Tract Society of New York, Inc., 1963.

Did Man Get Here by Evolution or by Creation? Brooklyn: Watchtower Bible and Tract Society of New York, Inc., 1963.

Equipped for Every Good Work. Brooklyn: Watchtower Bible and Tract Society, Inc., 1946.

From Paradise Lost to Paradise Regained. Brooklyn: Watchtower Bible and Tract Society of New York, Inc., 1958.

God's Kingdom of a Thousand Years Has Approached. Brooklyn: Watchtower Bible and Tract Society of New York, Inc., 1973.

Good News to Make You Happy. Brooklyn: Watchtower Bible and Tract Society of New York, Inc., 1976.

Holy Spirit: The Force Behind the Coming New Order. Brooklyn: Watchtower Bible and Tract Society of New York, Inc., 1976.

Is the Bible Really the Word of God? Brooklyn: Watchtower Bible and Tract Society of New York, Inc., 1969.

Jehovah's Witnesses in the Divine Purpose. Brooklyn: Watchtower Bible and Tract Society of New York, Inc., 1969.

The Kingdom is at Hand. Brooklyn: Watchtower

Bible and Tract Society of New York, Inc., 1944.

Let God Be True. Rev. ed. Brooklyn: Watchtower Bible and Tract Society, Inc., 1952.

Let Your Name Be Sanctified. Brooklyn: Watchtower Bible and Tract Society of New York, Inc., 1961.

Life Everlasting in Freedom of the Sons of God. Brooklyn: Watchtower Bible and Tract Society of New York, Inc., 1966.

Make Sure of All Things. Brooklyn: Watchtower Bible and Tract Society, Inc., 1953.

Make Sure of All Things, Hold Fast to What Is Fine. Brooklyn: Watchtower Bible and Tract Society of New York, Inc., 1965.

Making Your Family Life Happy. Brooklyn: Watchtower Bible and Tract Society of New York, Inc., 1978.

Man's Salvation out of World Distress at Hand! Brooklyn: Watchtower Bible and Tract Society of New York, Inc., 1975.

New Heavens and a New Earth. Brooklyn: Watchtower Bible and Tract Society, Inc., 1953.

New World Translation of the Holy Scriptures. Brooklyn: Watchtower Bible and Tract Society of New York, Inc., 1961.

Qualified to Be Ministers. Brooklyn: Watchtower Bible and Tract Society of New York, Inc. 1955.

Then Is Finished the Mystery of God. Brooklyn: Watchtower Bible and Tract Society of New York, Inc., 1969.

Things in Which It Is Impossible for God to Lie. Brooklyn: Watchtower Bible and Tract Society of New York, Inc., 1965.

This Means Everlasting Life. Brooklyn: Watchtower Bible and Tract Society, Inc., 1950.

The Truth Shall Make You Free. Brooklyn: Watchtower Bible and Tract Society, Inc., 1943.

The Truth That Leads to Eternal Life. Brooklyn: Watchtower Bible and Tract Society of New York, Inc., 1968.

What Has Religion Done for Mankind? Brooklyn: Watchtower Bible and Tract Society, Inc., 1951.

You May Survive Armageddon into God's New World. Brooklyn: Watchtower Bible and Tract Society, Inc., 1955.

Your Will Be Done on Earth. Brooklyn: Watchtower Bible and Tract Society of New York, Inc., 1958.

Watchtower Articles

"Aid to Bible Understanding." *The Watchtower* (November 1, 1975): 665.

"Appreciating Our Relationship with Jehovah." *The Watchtower* (May 15, 1975): 305–11

"A Book of Myths or a Misrepresented Guide?" *Awake!* (October 8, 1975): 10–11.

"A Capital for the Universe." *The Watchtower* (August 15, 1975): 490–92.

"The Death of a God." *The Watchtower* (May 1, 1975): 269–71.

"The Farmer and World Food Shortages." *Awake!* (June 22, 1975): 9–11.

"A Global Paradise—Why Possible?" *Awake!* (December 22, 1975): 4–8.

"How We Know God's Government Will Take Control Soon." *The Watchtower* (October 15, 1975): 632–35.

"Increasing Crime and Violence." *Awake!* (October 22, 1979): 3–4.

"Is Pollution God's Fault?" *Awake!* (July 8, 1975): 8–11.

"Is the Bible Realistic?" *Awake!* (October 8, 1975): 12–15.

"Kingdom Preaching—What Impact in Catholic Spain?" *The Watchtower* (August 1, 1975): 456–58.

"Millions Have Left the Churches—Should You?" *The Watchtower* (June 1, 1975): 323–26.

"One World, One Government, under God's Sovereignty." *The Watchtower* (October 15, 1975): 611–16.

"Our Refuge Under the Incorruptible 'Kingdom of the Heavens'." *The Watchtower* (November 15, 1975): 685–91.

"Paradise—A Desirable Place in Which to Live." *Awake!* (December 22, 1975): 3.

"Proving Ourselves Worthy to Enter God's New Order." *The Watchtower* (December 15, 1975): 745–51.

"Real Protection near at Hand!" *Awake!* (November 22, 1975): 14–16.

"The Time for Choosing God as Sovereign." *The Watchtower* (November 1, 1975): 658–63.

"What Is the Bible's View? Accept or Refuse Blood Transfusions?" *Awake!* (June 8, 1975): 27–28.

"What Is the Bible's View? What Is the Soul?" *Awake!* (August 8, 1975): 27–28.

"What Is the Bible's View? Will the Earth One Day Be Destroyed?" *Awake!* (August 22, 1975): 27–28.

"What the Churches Do Not Tell You." *The Watchtower* (June 15, 1975): 355–58.

"Why Such a Costly Ransom Price?" *The Watchtower* (July 15, 1975): 429–32.

"Will *You* See All the Earth Become a Paradise?" *Awake!* (December 22, 1975): 8–12.

"Your Soul." *The Watchtower* (December 15, 1975): 744.

Unpublished Works

Goodrich, Arthur Reddington. "Soteriology in Jehovah's Witnesses." Th.M. thesis, Dallas Theological Seminary, 1955.